A Maternal Awakening

by

Cheryl Norman Cordero

DORRANCE PUBLISHING CO
EST. 1920
PITTSBURGH, PENNSYLVANIA 15238

Dorrance Publishing Co
585 Alpha Drive
Pittsburgh, PA 15238
Visit our website at *www.dorrancebookstore.com*

ISBN: 979-8-89499-303-4
eISBN: 979-8-89499-802-2

Dedication

<hr>

This book is dedicated to my family, first and foremost. My mom, who spent her entire life making sacrifices for her kids, to my own kids, who are the reason for my being, to my cousin Stephen who died too soon, and to my husband with whom I plan to grow old with, overcoming the obstacles that are a part of life. I also want to give a special mention to all the misfits out there, who have walked the unbeaten path, always trying to stay true to themselves. And lastly, during editing, I found out that someone I had thought of as a son, one of my son's friends that I had tried to help for the past fourteen years, talking to him about his childhood traumas and drug addictions that had become a part of his everyday life, has sadly died. I got very close at times, to getting him into rehab, until his addictions would win, and have him chasing that high once again. He was found in Dolores Park on October 15th, a park that overlooks the entire city, where thousands of people go on weekends to enjoy the sun and hang out with friends. So, I know that he will forever be surrounded by love, friends, and peace, something that had eluded him here on earth. His spirituality was always intact, even though he had spent endless nights sleeping on the streets, stopping by often to ask for a blanket or a pair of clean socks.

Pepe, I only wish your life could have been a little kinder and gentler here on earth. "You were loved!"

Preface....

One day I stared at an angelic white duck swimming across a pond, as the sun glimmered on its back like white diamonds, while spiraling ripples fanned out behind her. As she glided along under the rays of the sun, two little baby ducklings trailed behind, ever so submissively. I watched as they all three danced in motion to the subtle waves that ebbed and flowed as mom proudly held her head high, as if keenly aware that the treasures that trailed behind her were her past, present, and future. And those are just what our offspring are. They are pieces of our past that have us nostalgic for our youth. They are our present that keep us grounded to the ever-changing roads we walk upon, and they keep us excited for a future unknown, that unfolds the mysteries in our lives and gives our dreams structure. I have three of my own, these creatures that stare back at me as if to say, "What am I supposed to do in these shoes, where shall I go from here?" And I stare back trying to retain my composure, knowing damn well that I have no idea, because in reality, we are all here without a manual. We were not given a playbook at birth to refer to when we need to plan our next move. We are all just drifters, drifting on an open sea of uncertainty, not really knowing where we came from, or where we are going. But we are all desperately trying to decipher the clues of the universe, while typically second guessing ourselves along the way. We all want to be right, and to remain silent, can be painful, when instinct has us wanting to shout our truths out loudly. We generally learn, through time, that whispers are usually sufficient. I decided to write a book about motherhood, because most of the books I have read did not really represent my story. Each step of my journey has felt like endless hurdles, obstacles so high, that I felt I needed countless ladders to overcome their height. There have been so many mistakes along the way, but so many triumphs as well, and at some point, that has to be good enough. Being a school bus driver for special-ed kids has taught me to love all kids, even those that are not my own, because everyday I get to see the innocence in their eyes, most not jaded yet by a life that is sure to disappoint. Everyday, I feel that I am giving them some takeaways, hoping they can take them to use as building blocks for their future, no matter how small or insignificant they might seem, but still attempting to make a small contribution just the same. I have struggled with addictions, anxieties, and childhood complexities that, at times, have left me on my knees struggling to not fall further down into the abyss. So my story is just that, and I will explain more here. It was never consciously my purpose to tell my story, but somehow it all intertwined together with the larger scale of the universe. I wanted to delve into all aspects of motherhood from earlier times to the present to uncover the mysteries of how we have interpreted motherhood throughout the years, and I went as far as to interview different people, men and women, to help me understand the issues surrounding it. Sometimes fathers are overlooked in the equation, so I added their voices as well. They too, especially in this day and age, are important players in the shaping of their child's lives, where in the past, they would have typically played smaller roles in the rearing of their children. In this somewhat memoir, that is not just my story, but the story of all parents. I address topics such as adoption, the inability to conceive, and being a single parent. I shared what it is like for a mother of an autistic child, her struggles with the unconventional, learning that parents of autistic children possess a uniqueness that brings challenges that still provide great rewards because we all have challenges in life and, overcoming them is undoubtedly hard, but nevertheless rewarding. I tried to leave no stone unturned. This story is not just my story but the story of all parents. More importantly, I wanted to analyze where we are going as a collective species, into the future that I feel is inevitably leading us into a new life cycle led by AI. I truthfully believe that it is too late to turn back because the ball has already been set in motion, rolling very fast down a hill of modern technology that will change the playing field altogether. I'm fully aware that AI offers us great opportunities in the fields of science and innovation, but I fear that we might be overtaken by its advances. Lately, I have seen so many important people, even the president, that have seemed worried about AI's rapid advances and question whether or not we are ready to be all encompassed by it, even holding meetings with tech giants to plead their concerns. At certain points my book becomes rather methodical, to the point of possibly lagging, yet I encourage you to take my lead so as to travel where I want you to go. The information I have shared is rather basic, more like a 101 refresher course, but I still find the simplest aspects of the formation of the universe fascinating. But in the end, this is your story because you have the ability to decipher your own meaning of life and, if you're a parent, you know the connection a parent has to their child, the struggles he or she faces on a daily basis, and how we are all perfectly imperfect living in our bodies of piled flesh.

I wrote this book over a span of two months, opening my little chromebook on breaks at work and sneaking in a few paragraphs with my morning coffee. Once in a while I would awaken at night and throw down a few ideas while half asleep because, you gotta do what you gotta do, and once I came up with the idea to write this book, it needed to be done immediately because that's how I take on new things in my life. I am always trying to push myself to keep moving along into my own future. I like putting new things in front of me to find purpose on this planet and to give myself motivation to keep on keeping on. Everyday I tumble through life like damp clothes in a dryer, clinging to warmth in a cold world that feels more like one big test than one big life. I've been a one man army, trekking through the trenches of existence with a determination to make it to the finish line. Everyday, everyone feels the struggle, and we do our best to distract ourselves from the monotony of 9 to 5 jobs, grocery store trips and the piles of bills by engaging for hours on social media, binge watching TV series, and engaging in distractions that allow us to make it through another day here on an unpredictable and unapologetic planet.

I have added some of my art, photography, and poetry because it's a part of who I am. If anyone is interested in listening to any of the bands I was in or music that I have made you could find me on Spotify under "Cheryl Ossola. No Place to Run," or on more punk albums I'm on, "The Nightcrawlers. Angel Alley" or "Squat. It's All Over." I will always find a way to be creative for the best chance of staying sane.

I also wanted to make clear that I tried to interpret all the interviewees I questioned to the best of my abilities and tried to convey their thoughts and opinions but everything conveyed to me was just that, an opinion, so if they are describing some situation or person it is from their point of view, and we all know there is more than just one point of view for every situation. I might have perceived what they said a little differently than they had meant but I tried hard to stick to the script and not interject my opinions during the interview. I will add that all my opinions are my own and are in no way the opinions of anyone I interviewed.

Also, I am not a rocket scientist, however, it would be ok if I were, because I would undoubtedly get paid better than I do in my current job. I'm basically someone that walked blindly through life for a long time and went from, walking on an obnoxiously curvy road, to a more cohesive straight and narrow one. For the most part, I am a boring person, but I will always have a wild side that wants to wander out there with no direction. I love getting in a car without a destination and just driving till I end up somewhere then trying to make the most out of that place and find some adventure in it. I think my point in saying this, is that there could be some facts in my book that are a little off. I tried my best to let you know as the reader when I am speculating or just hypothesizing about something and being that I started the book without a clear vision, as soon as the words hit the paper, I began to see the structure so some of it is written as a thought flowing process like I am doing right now. I can only hope that you enjoy it and walk away after having read it open minded to all things in life, to all possibilities, because there are no absolutes ever in life, and to be tolerant of other people's opinions and positions other than your own, because that's what life's all about, a give and take from one another. The giving and receiving of ideas and attitudes can not be underestimated. Can you imagine if we were all clones, all exactly the same with no imperfections and all the same political views, and any and all other views that seem to get scrutinized to death, allowing people to divide down lines without any chance for open-mindness that could lead to healthy discussions and, God forbid, maybe a change in your own point of view. Listening, contemplating, and sharing ideas is a beautiful thing so let's enjoy it now before we really are all the same when we become robotic AI type creatures that have done away with trivial emotions. And without any further ado…. Here are the pieces of my story, and possibly yours.

Walk into your future, with both eyes wide-open

My Dream:

Falling from the earth to the galaxies. Breaking
the universal barriers.

Tearing through the gravity that holds our souls
against the rough soil

Shattering the glass between the planets and the
stars. Acknowledging the myths that shaped and
caused our imaginations to erupt.

Awaiting to explore a new dimension To redefne
our term of existence.

Primitive Times.....

    But who am I but one of millions of females with thoughts and feelings on the subject of maternity. And like the tides that are affected by our sister moon, so are our menstrual cycles and emotions that ebb and flow with her ever-changing phases. Similar to a fetus, she emerges as a mere sliver of presence to transform into her wholeness engulfed like a full-term belly ready to give birth. Throughout time women have danced and sang at night under her mystical glow celebrating their womanhood. And so I embark on a journey to find out what it all means. To sit calm and quiet in a world that screams at us through rapidly changing technological advances. It is a challenge in itself, to find clarity, but I am challenging myself to make sense of my shifting views about pregnancy and motherhood. I will kiss ink to paper to explore all aspects of conceiving, discovering that there are many similar yet conflicting paths to take and never forgetting that pregnancy is, and has always been, a blessing to some while a curse to others. So let us begin this journey together.

So many aspects of motherhood. Even the steps ones takes to conceive have changed drastically from the beginning of humankind when we were more primal, women most likely having little choice than to succumb to men who were compelled by their biology to spread their seed to give life to a new generation, who in turn, reproduced to keep the cycle going. I'm always taken aback by Darwin's theory of the survival of the fittest because in those primitive times, life was based solely on the basic human needs for survival. Food, shelter, and the call to reproduce to carry on our races. To achieve that men had to not only strive to kill or be killed, they had to captivate their conquests. And women had to carry the fruit of the womb to fruition for the succession of their ancestral lineage.

From those earliest days this was not just a human trait. Other species developed through natural selection that would promise the continuance of their own species. From the simplest single-cell organisms grew more complex ones changing and adapting when it was necessary for their survival. Most of us were taught in school Darwin's example of the moths that change colors to blend into the trees, thus as to not be seen by their predators. Moths have a short gestation period allowing the natural selection process to work on a faster time scale. Darwin offered the theory that the Peppered moth was a perfect example of natural selection. The Peppered Moth whose lightly camouflaged frame freckled with black dots reduces her risk to become easy prey on the leaves of lichen covered tree trunks that stretch across europe by naturally blending in as opposed to the naturally occurring mutated variety known as melanic that are a black version making them quite a bit more visible than their counterpart. But during the Industrial Revolution factories polluted cities that housed these trees, charring some, while killing others. It was then that the mutated version prevailed because they blended into the blackened trees better and were less visible to their would-be captors giving them the advantage to reproduce making them the dominant ones. But as in life, change was around the corner and when Europe cleaned up its air pollution allowing the Lichen trees to rebound and make a comeback, the once prevalent black strand now were the ones on the chopping block and the lighter hued ones had the advantage to survive multiplying their breeding statistics and increasing their numbers as the melanic died off more quickly.

Darwin also realized that giraffes displayed the same benefits of natural selection because their long necks allowed them to reach for food that other animals could not get to that enabled them more chances to survive in environments where food was only accessible to those animals that could eat it from tall trees. Shorter animals without this trait might succumb to hunger because they were not able to attain the vegetation and fruits of the trees.

Evolution of modern humans derived from our earliest ancestors. The landscape of Africa that had once been lush with jungles had transformed into wide open savannahs. Chimps and apes that had spent much of their lives in trees hanging and swinging from limb to limb caring for their young and acquiring food now were reduced to wandering the wide open plains. Gone was the need for lanky arms and long curved fingers diminutive thumbs. These gave way to shorter arms and opposable thumbs that aided in tool making and locomotion. Natural selection would come into play to make life easier for the ever-evolving humanoid. Neanderthals still possessed the longer arms but gradually over time they would shorten into the homo-sapien era and the ever evolving species would be able to use their arms now to gather things they needed for shelter, grab food, and they even used them to make gestures as a form of communication. Over a great time span even their skeletons began to change. The structure of their knees, hips, and pelvic bones changed aiding to bipedalism which made it more easy for our ancient ancestors to walk long distances, to run and gather resources and to gather fruits and berries to eat, Walking upright with shorter arms took less energy and opened up a lot more opportunities that have led us into our modern state.

Mothers of all species are the building blocks of any society. We carry our young in our wombs for ten months giving rise to new generations. Some mothers lay their eggs and when they hatch a new life sprouts from the shell it had once incubated in. Such a miracle to be able to produce a new life and some mothers sacrifice everything to achieve this selfless gift. Pregnant mothers have their bellies swell like swollen thumbs until they pop like big balloons but the process is anything but simple and easy, moreover, it is confusing and scary. Getting up one morning to make your coffee and all of a sudden a gush of water comes pouring out of you and worse yet the panic sets in. Will I get to the hospital in time? Where is my packed bag? (The same one that was packed ever so carefully months ago but is now mysteriously missing.) And then the contractions start. At first so light that you start to wonder what all the fuss was about but in the hospital they become strong and violent while the bright lights of the delivery room blind you and the doctors cold gloves press against your body prodding and poking you like a raw piece of meat. And you lay on the table panting and reeling from the pain that seems to be unbearable like a locomotive streamlining out of your vagina. Pains and sensations you have never felt before unless you have already had a kid. And anyone who has had a kid knows that you forget this torture because no sane woman would ever let herself be impregnated again. Pain so bad that nausea sweeps over you as you wail and moan like a wounded animal that's been struck by a hunters bullet. And finally those words that you've been waiting to hear til you actually start doing it. "Push, Push!," as your breathing becomes rushed and you feel outta breath. The contractions wreak havoc on your brevity that you once had sitting at home calmly reading about how to breathe and let yourself go with the waves of contractions as you sip your chamomile tea. You are pissed off even thinking you could have thought this was going to be some modern liberating feat that has now turned into, "You versus the world," or so it seems. All the while doctors yelling at you to push and nurses holding your legs as if the more they tug the harder you'll push. And the tearing, could it really get worse? So now you have been reduced to an animalistic monster who has no problem cussing at the doctors to make it stop and assuring your husband or partner that this is all their fault until finally, as sweat pools off your face, and your legs tremble from pain, you cant push anymore, you give one last ditch effort and breathe in like you never have before, and push and exhale like you're blowing out 2000 candles, and then it happens. The baby releases itself from your womb and welcomes itself into the world. You lock eyes with him or her and you know that you have just birthed a new life into this world. And life as you knew it, would never be the same Throughout time, most women have proven to be the fiercest warriors who will stop at nothing to protect their young. Having just described the birthing process, it's obvious that they are super-women with super-powers. However, the animal kingdom produces some of the bravest and most hard working moms on the planet.

The polar bear is a prime example of a mom that gives her all for the well-being of her cubs. She feeds on seals for months at a time to retain the necessary fat that she will need to carry her throughout the entirety of her pregnancy. Her milk that she'll produce is 31% fat and a lot of preparation must go into achieving this amount. After she mates, she digs a den in the ice where she'll spend the next several months hibernating waiting for the arrival of her babies. Usually born in pairs, the cubs come into the world with little hair and eyes clenched shut, not ready to face the world around them. They are completely reliant on her abilities as a mother to provide them with the care that they will need for the next couple of years. She'll spend four to six months in the den tending to her new arrivals who will deplete her fat reserve. Starving, she will instinctively know that she must leave her safe haven and lead the cubs out into the dangerous elements. Trucking through thick ice and snow she often has to carry them on her back and stop often for feedings until reaching frigid waters, where she will teach them to hunt for food, protect them from older bears that could cause them harm, watch over them while they learn to swim making sure they don't drown, navigate sea-ice, and adapt and prosper in the cold Arctic environment. As soon as her cubs reach adulthood, the bears can fend for themselves and the exhausting process for the polar bear mother begins all over again, most averaging about eight litters in a lifetime. An endless cycle that ensures the future of polar bears by giving them the greatest chances of survival in such a harsh climate.

The octopus is but one more example of the links that a mom will go to to give birth to the next generation, often making the greatest sacrifice of all, herself. If you've ever watched "My Octopus Teacher," you will witness one of the most magical stories ever put up on the silver screen. The star is a cephalopod that is befriended by a man who captures her beauty and evolution on film. Through his lens and over time they form a shocking and unexpected bond as he captures beautifully as her plight of motherhood becomes a reality. The cinematography is breathtaking as we move with her through coral reefs and marvel at her ability to camouflage herself changing shapes and colors to avoid being seen and killed. At one heartbreaking point in the movie, she is attacked by a shark and loses one of her tentacles, but in time she miraculously recovers. Her tenacity has you spellbound and as she mysteriously roams the ocean waters alone traveling for what seems an eternity searching for a mate to reproduce. Instinctively after being impregnated, she lays in wait under rocks, sitting on her precious eggs guarding them for sometimes up to an unthinkable four years. Sadly, cephalopods generally succumb to starvation and die but their selfless sacrifices are what gives rise to the birth and continuance of the species. We are moved to tears watching her last moments overwhelmed with emotion witnessing her seemingly lonely existence solely to reproduce and the painstaking steps she took for her babies.

One last example of a mother's dedication are elephants, who are a perfect example of, "It takes a village," in regards to rearing kids. They live in a matriarchal society with aunts, moms, sisters, and grandparents all teaming up to raise thebabies. Multi-generational knowledge that can only be learned over time and through experience is passed down the pipeline of these gentle giants with younger generations learning from those who came before them. Elephants are highly intelligent creatures with amazing memories and the elders in the group use their social and cultural memory to teach the younger generations. An example of this, would be a drought that had killed off many of the elephants in the past, would be remembered by the senior elephants of the herd and they would remember where to find the last ditch water reserve from surviving the event before.

They are the largest of the land mammals on Earth but are filled with empathy and love. When one of their own dies there is a morning process that is ceremonial in nature. Some even rock their babies to sleep at night and the group teaches the growing kids to stand, swim, and how to find food. So nurturing in fact, that they walk in a single file line trunk to tail to ensure the safety of the younger ones. These angelic creatures have hearts of gold. Fiercely nurturing females bond together to oversee the little ones that have come into their matriarchal group and, I believe that on this, they should be commended.

So Darwin's theory of natural selection is seen throughout all species, some evolving slowly while others evolving quickly and some dying off altogether. But Darwin wasn't done yet, he went on to theorize that not only was there natural selection, but he added the cherry on top, the tantalizing cherry you lick and devour, and added that sexual selection plays A part as well. And how could it be denied, when sexual drive is such a torrential force of nature that has living things going to any links to reproduce. The theory has two parts, interspecies and intraspecies. The first suggests that same sex members of a species fight and compete with one another for the ability to mate with the opposite sex and the other that they gain attributes through this process that will help them attract the opposite sex. A peacock was used as a perfect example because obviously a long luxurious peacock tail does not make sense as a natural selection trait because it would deter him from surviving capture however it would indeed attract the attention of a female peacock thus giving it an advantage to mate and, in turn, increasing its chances to reproduce. So sexual selection is the key element in ensuring a chance to produce future offspring. A deer displays sexual selection in the size of his antlers because he will use these to fight for a member of the opposite sex to be able to mate and carry on his genes. Males are always adapting through mutation to appear more appealing to the opposite sex. They will be more desirable the stronger and bulkier they get while female admirers choose who they will mate with based on these dominant male characteristics.

Male Manakin birds will try to outperform each other preparing dances that they spend months if not years practicing just for the one chance to perform in front of their female conquest trying desperately to win her affection. They will practice relentlessly to learn their trademark moonslide dance on a tree branch till they eventually slide effortlessly back and forth, clicking and snapping, making it clear to their onlookers that they, and not Michael Jackson, are actually the ones who invented the moonwalk. Animals continue the fine balance of mutating through sexual selection until their ornamental features render them unable to survive and at some point they will need to reel their fancy attributes back in so sexual selection doesn't completely override natural selection and they won't be killed off in the environments they occupy. There's nothing sexy about getting killed by a member of your own sex when you're trying to get your groove on.

In the animal kingdom, females are almost always the ones choosing their mates. Occasionally males are the ones who will choose but that would coincide with the fact that they were the ones looking after the eggs and embryos. In some bird breeds, the female will actually leave her egg with her mate making him the caregiver of the offspring and this leads to her being the one that tries to acquire the attention of her conquest by mutating her genes till she shines with beauty by adding bright colorful feathers to her flock and singing songs to attract the males for attention. It seems relatable that humans have coexisted with these animals and women too have played the same role, choosing males based on sexual attributes, while men tried to show off their strengths, talents, and accomplishments though that seems to be, in current times, changing with the roles becoming blurred.

Coming Into More Civilized Times......

Over time things changed when the hunters and gatherers gained knowledge and civilizations sprung up with different peoples settling along rivers in the Middle East and Asia. The Egyptians began occupying the land that rests on the banks of the Nile River. In Mesopotamia, The Assyrians, Sumerians, Akkadians, and Babylonians were living between the Tigris and Euphrates Rivers or in the vicinity thereof. There was a new civilization beginning in the Indus Valley in modern day Pakistan and, in China the Shangs were building a dynasty on the Yangtze River. Life was accelerating, propelling forward but still they were far from modern times. All these peoples began to cluster along the rivers that would give life to their families; the kings, queens, pharaohs, and unfortunately, the slaves that they would use to do their most labor intensive work. They learned to cultivate crops and domesticate animals and, for the first time in history, these locations were flourishing like never before, and in turn, creating a class system. Where there'd been herders moving around to where there was food to be scavenged, there were now stationary peoples living in settlements with an abundance of food to store for reserves during dryer seasons. This food abundance opened up a new lifestyle. Men and women carried out specialized jobs now. Some made clay pots used to store food, some were artisans building structures as grand as the Pyramids with tools and their bare hands, and others worked as scribes using symbols such as Cuneiform to help their people trade and communicate with one another. Some women of wealth had servants to help care for the kids. Separation of wealth created wealthy households and most certainly a middle class while slaves were used where needed or with jobs they didn't want to do themselves. In this new existence men and women most likely shared a new type or relationship.

Now that men were most likely staying home more, not out on some extended hunt, while women bonded together protecting the young, I would assume that there would have been a new type of bond between the husband and wife where they would be working more as as team that would more resemble a modern day family unit with the dad playing a slightly larger role in the rearing of a child.

For the first time in history a real trade network began. Jade, silk, and spices were all being transported on new trade routes to other civilized peoples where their languages and cultures crossed paths creating cross-cultures, a somewhat giving and taking of one's ideas and new ways of life. All this new prosperity and opportunity created wars leading the Assyrians, Babylonians, Sumerians, and Hittites to battle one another for power in their territories whilst the Shangs of China, who were more isolated by the mountains and ocean, battled each other for power in a more Civil War type archetype, but times were tumultuous and the landscape moved to and fro like earthquakes rumbling through territories with different rulers being wiped out by other kings and territorial lines being uprooted and changed across the continents. One constant though, was that babies were still being born into the world and, now more than ever, the people looked to the night skies for clarity to make sense of their overwhelming new surroundings. The myths that shaped and caused their imaginations to erupt were the backbone of these new civilized peoples. Their Deities differed across the cultures but shared similar traits.

The Mayans too developed a new civilization years later but only were truly recognized in 1839 when Federick Catherwood and John Lloyd Stevens made detail drawings of over 44 Mayan settlements in precise detail on their extended expedition to Central America, Chiapas and the Yucatan to give the western world a birds eye view into the life of the Mayans. It is believed now that there were likely 15 to 20 million of them spread out around the jungles of Guatalahara and all of Yucatan Peninsula, much more than previously thought. Their ruins indicate they were a very complex civilization flourishing in tropical jungles and they had a taste for art and architecture, were advanced in math, and were in tune with astrological systems. Later surveys revealed that the Mayans had possibly the first ever super highways that allowed people of the time to travel to and from the different sites. Their fertility deity Ixchelwas known in Mayan mythology as the daughter of the creator god Itzamna and the mother of the sun god Kinich Ahau. She was considered the protector of pregnant women and newborns. At some time between A.D. 900 to 1100 they all mysteriously moved on from these astounding temples and all of what they had built. Theories have been proposed for reasons of their abandonment from wars to plaques to drought. The most interesting hypothesis though is that it was more a combination of misfortunes because things were not going so well leading up to the civilizations demise. They had created the Mayan calendar and it illustrates how they believed in life cycles, moreover, that everything had a beginning as well as an end and that at the completion of the cycle things would die off and the ashes from the past would create a new beginning, a rebirth if you will. So if they had perceived that their lives were not going well and that it coincided with the end of a cycle on their calendar that would have been enough of a prophecy to move on to new lands leaving behind their old lives to the jungles that would eventually consume and devour them swallowing them up with tree overgrowth causing the remnants of their distant past to fade away into secrecy until they were rediscovered.

The Anasazi, whose ancestors would rather they be referred to as the "Ancestral Puebloans," gave rise to some of the first civilized people in the United States around about 1400 years ago much later than the than people of Mesopotamia, that is also referred to as "The Fertile Crescent" and "The Cradle of Mankind." The Hopi and Pueblo Indians are said to be direct descendents of these tribal people. These people lived in what was called the Four Corners consisting of New Mexico, Colorado, Arizona, and Utah. They too, like the Mayans in the South, mysteriously disappeared and rather abruptly leaving behind pottery and other items as if they picked up and just left. They were a sophisticated people some living in Great Houses that were built with multistories some even containing up to 800 rooms while others lived in cave dwellings carved in rocks and caves to keep them cool from the hot and non-forgiving New Mexico sun in a place named Cliff Palace in Mesa Verde National Park. Their fertility deity was named Kokopelli who is depicted as a humpbacked flute player often with feathers or antenna-like protrusions on his head and presides over both childbirth and agriculture. Kokopelli is not alone because there are countless fertility Gods spanning over many societies differing in appearance and meaning. The African goddess of fertility is Ala. She rules over the underworld and holds the deceased ancestors in her womb. Asase Ya is the Akan goddess of fertility in Ghana and the Ivory Coast. Deng is a sky, rain, and fertility god for the Dinka people of Sudan and South Sudan. In the Dinka religion he is a storm and fertility god who brings lighting rain and thunder. Oshun is the goddess of divinity, femininity, fertility, beauty and love. In Egypt there were many goddesses associated with fertility; Amun, Bastet, (a cat goddess of fertility), Heqet (a frog goddess of fertility), Heryshaf, Isis, Knum, Messenet, (A goddess of childbirth,) and Min (God of reproduction) and many, many more. The Incas had Mama Ocllo, The Inuits had Akna, The Aztecs had Chimalma and Xochipilli. Cultures relied on these goddesses to guide them through pregnancy and bless them with a healthy child. Aphrodite is one of the most well known fertility goddesses but collectively they are associated with sex, pregnancy, women's fertility, and the growing of crops.

The Anasazi culture was somewhat unique in that the woman chose their mate or man that they would marry and then they would go to his parents to ask for approval. However at some point they too picked up and left leaving anthropologists baffled not exactly sure why they abandoned their dwellings but the same guesses are at play with drought and disease being on the suggestion list however some think that they were scared off by a folklore tale that spoke of a "Gambler" who, as folklore would have it, had them building their settlements just to reduce them to his slaves until they came to believe he was overstepping his bounds and they ran him off. As the story continued, he cursed the whole town, attributing to their departure outta fear they were cursed and doomed by the Gambler and would never return to the area.

I can only imagine what it might have been like for all of those living in these earliest civilizations, outside of city lights, before iPhones became people's Gods. What these ancient people must have thought when they looked up into the abyss of the night sky, marveled at that ever-changing moon, gazed into the kaleidoscope of lights, and marveled at a sun that traveled like a motorized ball traveling east to west before disappearing into nothingness. Men and women standing on different shores and mountaintops but still seeing the same sea of endless stars, exploding at times. They must have perceived them to be arrows being shot from a God's bow, while meteorites crisscrossed from above like cannons from angry sky warriors, and planets glowed like precious jewels from apparent wealthier planets out in a mysterious universe. Bewildering it must have been, to look out into the unknown not knowing if you were living on a flat planet under a glass globe controlled by far away Gods. So they were free to imagine. Everyday was doused with magic from the sun gods, moon gods, animal gods, and of course, fertility gods. Mysticism was a way to explain the unknown from people wanting to make sense of their all encumbersome world.

These were a polytheistic peoples who believed in an array of Gods. Everything tangible was what was real to them. When a river failed to flood during the wet season and water became a problem, in their minds, this was a punishment from the Gods and they would then give human sacrifices to try and redeem themselves from their past wrongdoings, sometimes using innocent babies as offerings.

Our accounts of history have slowly changed over time and anthropologists and historians have reluctantly, when pressured enough, moved the goalposts back to allow for discrepancies in different historical timelines and events from our past. So even in writing this, I am aware that my timeline could be askew. There might have been civilizations going back much farther than I seem to theorize. Aliens could have been here long ago, after all there are almost identical structures they have found in places where people supposedly had no contact with one another and some questioned how the Egyptians could have built the pyramids so precisely and suggested alien beings gave them the knowledge it took to create them. Graham Hancock has suggested that our first civilization goes back much further than previously thought when a shepherd discovered a new archaeological site in Turkey called Gobekli Tepe. Carbon dating dates the site as existing over 12,000 years ago right after the last ice age. This would predate the Egyptians and those living in Mesopotamia. Some stand firm that these were just hunters and gathering peoples but it seems quite plausible that these people were more civilized than the skeptics would like to admit. In fact, ancient civilizations are often interpreted by anthropologists who often can only speculate because there were no iphones being held up recording every waking moment for a Tik-Tok post. No reality TV cameras following people around recording them breathing in every breath of their life. There were only oral accounts passed down from many generations and most likely embellished so much so, that they became entirely different stories altogether. And throughout time we have seen myths that seem to have been borrowed from earlier times in history. The great flood myths are depicted across many cultures as great devastating acts sent from divine deities for retribution to destroy mankind. Even before the well known Christian flood that had Moses gathering up animals on his arc, there were tales long before. In Ancient Egypt, the god Ra sent his daughter Sekhmet to destroy humanity with a flood for their disrespect and unfaithfulness. The flood-myth motif occurs in many cultures, including the Mesopotamia flood stories, the Native American flood story had a man named Waynboozhoo surviving a great flood that was sent by "The Creater" by building a raft out of floating sticks for the animals and himself enabling them to float around waiting for a full moon that would allow for the waters to recede, the Genesis flood narrative, manvantara-sandhya in Hinduism, and Deucalion and Pyrrha in Greek mythology. You have tales of the flooding of Atlantis by a great deluge that were shared through Plato's words but the mystery still remains of its location. But the question remains to many historians and anthropologists whether any of these great flood tales that wind and sift through time-spans and locals are truly describing the flood in the Bible or just devastating floods that toppled a region killing off thousands of people and destroying cities in times predating Noah's flood. As stories are passed on over generations by word of mouth, do they gain steam and eventually become bigger stories such as a local flood turning into a global event? This theory seems rather alluring to someone like Graham Hancock who has argued that the Biblical flood could have actually been a remnant of a past great flood myth. The Epic of Gilgamesh dates back 5,000 years and is thought to be one of the oldest tales to date. In the tale Utnapishtim is warned of a great flood from angry Gods and so he builds a circular-shaped boat that carries his relatives, animals, and grain, and like Noah in Genesis, he releases a bird in search of dry land. In Vedic lore, a fish tells the mythic king Manu of an eminent catastrophic flood that will wipe out humanity then leads him to a mountaintop for reprieve after building a boat to withstand the storm.

Also the story of Adam and Eve has been seen in previous myths before the Bible. The myth of Adam and Eve is a revision of older agrarian matriarchal myths, where the Mother Goddess has her place near the Tree of Life, a tree that is housed by a serpent (representing eternal life from the shedding of it's skin) and she offers fruit to the believer. Moving from a matriarchal society to a Hebrew patriarchal society the story changed from a female goddess to a mere human and changed from a salvation giving character to a salvation taking character because women needed to be perceived inferior to men in a patriarchal society and therefore she became the sinner. In the tale of Gilgamesh, Enkidu was a wild man who lived with the beasts and similarly mirrored the idyllic Adam pre-fall. To be lured outta paradise, a prostitute was sent to tempt him and the plan worked because after he had sex with her he was no longer able to understand the animals and they all fled. So much of life is interpretation and scholars have spent years trying to interpret myths of the past trying to tie different stories together like a mixed-match patch quilt looking for similarities across the cultures. It is up to individuals to decide their own truths and belief systems that have religions guiding their moral values. We are inevitably on our own personal journeys on this plain and we can choose to believe in the tales like Adam and Eve word for word or base it loosely on our perceptions of what we believe our values should be. Some who are atheists, don't believe there is any truth to any of it and dismiss any claims otherwise. Others believe that as in Hebrews 11:1, "Now faith is confidence in what we hope for and assurance about what we do not see." The Good News: Faith is based on trusting that God will not abandon you or you in a situation that's too tough to handle. This is repeated in every twelve-step program of recovery where they tell you that God will not give you anything that you can't handle and some believe that sometimes the toughest situations in your life are actually gifts from God to help you grow as a human being. They suggest that we must tap into our inner strength and not be negatively affected by the trials and tribulations even when they bring us to our knees because we can own that inner strength and/or faith that will eventually lead us out of the darkness into the light. A simulation of a re-birth some imply. So again, our personal journeys are ours and ours alone and one must address his or her own personal demons and be true to oneself and as **J.R.R.** Tolkien states "Not all that wander alone are lost."

Religious and spiritual beliefs are very personal to every individual and no one should pass judgement on those that believe something diffrent than themselves. Your path to walk is yours, and yours alone, but I will share here that I had an out of body experience when I was younger and have since learned that Psychedelics are know for inducing altered states of consciousness in humans by fundamentally changing our normal pattern of sensory perception, thought and emotion. When I was about 13 or 14 my neighbors son chaperoned me to a rock concert at the state fair grounds. As soon as we got there, we got in line with all the other concert goers when someone randomly gave both of us a hit of acid commonly known as L.S.D. I had no idea what it was at the time but took it anyways. As soon as the concert started the drug began to take affect. All of a sudden I was hunched over spitting on the ground and that's right when I literally was out of my body looking at myself doing this from about ten feet away. A few people had circled around me to see if I was ok and I was part of that same group watching myself from afar. I later learned that people use L.S.D. to try to experience this out of consciousness state but I believe that my ignorance of the drug enabled the drug to do what some take it for without any inhibitions getting in the way. I do not believe this was any type of hallucination because it was very clear and real. I believe that our souls are differently a part of us and that our bodies are only the vehicles in which they travel. Everyone should be entitled to belive in any God, Prophet or Messiah of their choosing, or none at all, without the damnation from others because, if they are true believers, they should know that they will not be the ones to cast judgement in the end. The mysteries of the universe are endless and we are all seekers trying to unlock locked doors to unravel it's truths.

Goddesses, Sirens, and Monsters...
The Women of Antiquity.....

My painting Siren's Under a Moonlit Night

As the curtain closed on the Hellenistic era with the death of Alexander the Great in 323 BCE an encore performance began with antiquity in ancient Greece and Rome and what a spectacular show it was. Alexander had been one of the greatest conquerors of all time, attaining territories as far as Asia to the East and Egypt to the West and all along the Eastern Mediterranean. He had been tutored by Aristotle and had wanted what the Persians had so he set off on his horse Bucephalus to achieve his aspirations. He conquered all of Mesoptopamia as well as Egypt and went undefeated in battle. As we look back in history we see the pattern clearly. If someone wanted what someone else had, whether it be land, riches, women, or whatever the booty might be, there was someone or some group of people ready to kill and conquer them to take what wasn't theirs. I'm sure stemming all the way back to the beginnings, there would have been tribes less productive at hunting or maintaining self-sufficiency and they would have viewed others with more food or a more hospitable territory as prey. They would have gathered their people and attacked hoping to obtain whatever riches the other one had, killing off whoever stood in their way. There have been no rules to the game and it's still going on to this very day as we've seen with the war in Ukraine where Russia is trying to pushback Ukranians for lost territories and whatever other factors they deem excusable while at the same time destroying beautiful buildings, killing innocent people and disrupting nature by setting off bombs and explosives into the atmosphere. Unfortunately, ego's and money typically drive these entities to plunder indiscreetly. There have been so many conquerors throughout time steamrollering over entire civilizations taking whatever they wanted and killing everyone in their way including children, many times raping the women and enslaving entire families. It's sad but true and I believe this will be the reality moving into the future unless AI eliminates through technology; the drive, desire and need to destroy others to gain more for themselves or to survive. Our evolution has brought us to a point where we can analyze the past like we hadn't before. Over the years the government has made some amends to the Native Americans for taking their land though more could be done. We are on a course that will hopefully give reparations to the African Americans whose families lines include slavery that would never have been done in our ancient history. Baby steps are being taken that will hopefully turn into big strides but unfortunately there will still be new wars waged in the future for the same old reasons. Humans seem to gravitate towards violence. We have, as a species, reveled in bloodsports cheering on Gladiators like Spartacus and Marcus Atillius Regulus who entertained Roman audiences with violent confrontations with other gladiators, wild-animals and criminals. Spectators in the colosseum couldn't get enough bloodshed watching them fight to their deaths. Pok-A-Tok was an ancient Mayan ball game that, at times, was used as a means to settle conflicts between warring groups and noblemen and spectators were fully aware that the losing side's leader or whole team might be sacrificed and killed. Jousting was a popular medieval sport that had two combatants attempting to knock his opponent off his horse. The lance used to strike was 15 to 25 pounds and, being struck with one while a horse was galloping at you at up to 30 m.p.h., could most certainly pierce an opponent sending him flying off his horse while onlookers cheered on the outskirts. One could be seriously injured or killed in this brutal sport. Henry VIII succumbed to an injury leading to his untimely death while jousting in 1559 when a lance pierced through his helmet, ripping into his face and neck. The longest spike tore into his right eye penetrating his brain while all the commoners looked on including his wife Catherin de' Medici of France. And even now, we still have a thirst for violence and blood. We gather round our Tv's every Sunday to watch football players tackle other players aggressively and linesmen crash into each other like mac trucks. We pay hundreds of dollars for pay-per-view events that have us watching the meanest and toughest boxers fighting one another. Spectators sit in the audience screaming for one of them to knock out the other one while blood oozes from their faces and sweat pools from their foreheads. We are not satisfied until blood is drawn but, at times, we may have our limits like when the world was taken aback and faces grimaced when Mike Tyson bit off a piece of Holyfield's ear. We were all in up until that point, then everyone watching at home with their fellow partiers, looked at each other like "Ah hell no, that ain't right." Mix-martial arts matches are just more events where people circle around a stage whose sport is solely based on two people beating the crap outta one another. Some have suggested that violent sports fill a void in the human psyche that was at one time filled with hunting and combat when men were warriors, and that throughout history, we have replaced this with games of violence and death that satisfies some sort of primal need or lust.

Throughout the centuries we've witnessed many tyrants taking over other territories and peoples. You have read about Attilla the Hun who was the most feared enemy of the Western and Eastern Roman Emperors. "The whole breadth of Europe… was at once invaded, and occupied and desolated, by the myriads of barbarians who Attilla led into the field," wrote Edward Gibbon in *The Decline and Fall of the Roman Empire*. He plundered and pillaged everything in his path. There was Ghenis Khan who actually left a mountain of skulls in China. He was the ruler of the biggest empire in history ruling over the Mongols and decimating anyone who got in his way leading to alarming population declines in conquered areas due to the brutality and from famine caused by the sweeping dissemination. Anywhere from four million on the low side, to a whooping sixty million people were estimated to have been killed during his military campaigns which are astonishing figures. Cyrus the Great of Persia occupied the largest empire of his time occupying The Four Corners of the World that encompassed Southwest Asia, Central Asia, and the Caucasus. You had Timur, Hannibal Barca, Pharaoh Thutmose III, and in modern times Adolf Hitler, Napoleon Bonapart, and Julias Caesar, and even The Vikings and Pirates of the Caribbean could be thrown into the mix. There have been so many tyrants and warriors whom some glorify as brave and skilled leaders and fighters while others look to them as horrible evil dictators and emperors and their armies that used their power to destroy. Yet, if we look at it through the eyes of evolution, the animal kingdom too, acts in the same way. Lions have a pride and when the male in the group gets too old he is removed from the pride by younger males from outside his pride claiming stake to his territory and his female pursuits. Sometimes the killing happens within communities instead of heading into enemy territory with factions from within like in the case of Foudouko, a West African Chimpanzee that was stoned and beaten to death with sticks by his own community because there were more adult males than females so the older male tyrant had to be killed off to secure the succession of younger male bloodlines. In the animal kingdom, chimpanzees do go to war fighting off other chimpanzee gangs to gain territory. To see this behavior you must watch the Chimp Empire to witness all the realities in the chimp world including their aim to conquer nearby chimps. It's a visual masterpiece allowing you access to chimps' lives from the comfort of your own couch. Ants, too, raid other colonies, sometimes even taking slaves. So we must keep this in mind when analyzing one's desire to seek and destroy other living things as part of a genetic drive. Hunger, thirst, wealth, repopulation and fertile lands can be so paulable that it can wet the lips of desire on any living organism with DNA.

And, while editing this book, a war has broken out between Israel and Palestine. It has made it hard to finish the edit because it sickens me that humans can be so deliberately cruel. We have seen the aftermath of men who were in their most savage state, indiscreetly killing entire families, burning some alive, and beheading others. Infants were not even exempt from the cruelty. Modern times have not yielded kinder and gentler wars or peaceful warriors. When men lose their sensibility because their emotions have prevailed, there is no limit to their savagery. And the real victims are the children who get caught up in the upheaval. They should be out playing soccer in the streets, engaging with friends, not hiding in shelters and watching as their parents are picked off by assault rifles and entire generations must leave everything they know to become refugees. Hamas began the destruction when they attacked innocent people in Israel, and now Israel has taken revenge by attacking innocent civilians in the Gaza Stript. "So, do two wrongs make a right?" I don't believe so. But throughout our history there has always been a tit for tat. The taste of revenge, as sweet as wine, but leaves you with a bittersweet hangover. We get lost in the events, and forget that we are all human beings, breathing and existing on one soil. Though our belief systems are different, there are more similarities than differences. "Why can't we stop to smell the flowers? Why can't we find wisdom in the trees? Why can't we float on an endless oceanic wave of peace, fully understanding that we are all one flowing soul that ebbs and flows throughout our atmosphere? How can we do this to the children?" We bring them into the world just so they can watch us blow it up in front of their innocent eyes. Eyes that want to see birds crisscrossing the skies above them, not missiles of death that have been sent to them from their neighbors. They want to run free in fields of wildflowers, not running from piercing bullets that leave them in their own pooling blood on soil that they called home. Parents want to be coddling their infants to make sure they are not getting injured, instead of witnessing their heads being cut off by some unfamiliar evil face of a man they have never met. "Yes, children are the victims!" There is a glitch in our DNA. One that allows us to justify this onslaught of human life, the dismantling of an entire people that mirror images from the Holocaust. "And for what gain?" So one can move into an area that has been completely destroyed. Infrastructure built by human hands, tired aching hands, tinged with colors of the clay of the earth. Men and women, who have worked tirelessly creating neighborhoods that had men building the structures, while women relied on their femininity to create warm and structured homes, and taught their kids about their heritage and culture. At one time, smells of rising bread rose from bakeries filling neighborhoods that now lay in rubble, rabbi's and Muslim leader's voices were carried by the winds of tradition, down long corridors, that now serve as graves for lives taken too soon, and once blue skies that promised a tomorrow, now a smoky gray, leaving doubt and uncertainty for any future solution for peace. "Should we destroy the beauty of nature and undo the doing of men's hands that have built family homes and temples? Should children be taught of a holy God and what it means to be a good human being, while at the same time watching their teachers blow up everything and kill everyone they know?"

We have also just watched the same thing go on between Ukraine and Russia, not for the same reasons, but again man destroying the beauty that was given to him by any means possible. This has created a diaspora with many fleeing the hostile environments for calmer areas in neighboring countries such as Poland. Women sitting on the cold pavement with crying children, whose identities have been stripped away from them in a blink of an eye. Families looking disheveled, trying to find meaning with their new found existence, that had them leaving behind all traces of their past, only to wonder what kind of future awaits them. Volunteers stood by the borders of Ukraine, day and night, and their cold hands trembled while they served up soup rations with a ladle. Mothers stood in lines waiting for donated jackets and baby diapers, unsure where they would sleep at night or if they would ever return home.

Also in recent times, another diaspora occurred when we withdrew our troops from Afghanistan and people fled for their lives, hanging from moving jetliners and throwing their babies over walls to strangers hoping they would have a better life.

Thousands of refugees landed here on American soil, being dispersed throughout the country, like goods off a boat. These families left behind everything they knew in their homeland, and now are living in towns across America trying to assimilate to a new way of life.

And this desire to conquer, be right, gain land, and territories, and the goodies that come with this pillaging, is deep seeded within us. We will only find a solution if we can find a way to wash this out of our DNA.

After a few insignificant rulers in Egypt, Ptlotomy, who had been one Alexander's generals, was named Pharaoh of Egypt and he created a dynasty of Greek speaking rulers that lasted almost 300 years until it fell to Rome at the battle of Corinth in 146 bc. The rise of the Roman republic lasted a span of 1000 years with its great fall in 476 by a barbarian named Odoacer who deposed the last Roman emperor Romalus Augustus.

Also, at the tail end of the Hellenistic period, lived A woman like no other who had been ruler of Egypt. Cleopatra, by now a household name, should not and will not be forgotten to history. She was the daughter of Ptolemy XII Auletes and the last Macedonian queen of Egypt. She used her female seductiveness, wit and persuasiveness to overcome the male-dominant world of the time protecting

Egypt and setting the stage for more powerful female leaders of the future like Empress Theodora who was the Empress of Byzantium, Amalasuntha Queen of the Goths, Joan of Arc who had led an army to war, Princess Olga of Kiev, and the ever famous Queen Elizabeth I who was the last of the Tudor Monarchs who never married and never had children referring to herself as 'wedded to the nation.' Cleopatra had to be ruthless at times even killing members of her own family and was able to seduce two of the most powerful men of the time Julias Caesar and Mark Antony uniting Rome and Egypt while ensuring Egypt's independence and bolstering Egypt's status as a World Power.

Rome eventually defeated the Greeks in 146 BC at the Battle of Corinth and Greece became part of the Roman Empire. The Roman empire included areas around the Mediterranean Sea in Europe, North Africa and Western Asia ruled by emperors such as its first emperor Caesar Augustus. Rome was in all ways a patrilocal society with the paterfamilias, who was the oldest male in a family, as the leader of the family unit. The men had complete control over their wives who were authorized and even encouraged to beat if they stepped outta line. It was believed that it was the males right to rule the household out of virtue. At times husbands took on relationships outside of the marriage with unwed women and males who would generally be on the younger side. They had freedoms women would never experience like voting and holding office. Women were also forbade from having a voice in public life and not allowed at public assemblies. Most elite men even took on more than one wife but the fidelity of the wife was expected. Men were legal citizens yet the women were only considered citizens through the extension of their husbands or fathers. Needless to say, most relationships were not bloomed out of deep affections but rather grew outta the desire for political advantages set forth by older relatives that stood to gain from the pairing and to cement alliances within two families and many times, great age differences made the union even more difficult. Many times the females would be married at 12 and 13 years old leading to them having 4 or 5 kids by the time they were twenty often resulting in their death. Women of Rome were either midwives, goddesses, priestesses, empresses, prostitutes, or possibly store owners or clerks. To ensure urgency, Augustus even passed a law that heavily penalized women over the age of 20 who were unmarried. So these young women were but mere political pawns whose main focus was to tend to the home and spin thread and weave clothing and to be subordinate to their husbands. Most importantly though, they were expected to bear as many children as possible. Their offspring would ensure that the Gods would continue to be worshiped.

Motherhood in these times was very dangerous for the woman and the child. Women were encouraged to lay in bed before the birth to preserve the seed. Midwives were there to assist with the preparation of the upcoming birth by lubricating her for a smooth birth and massaging them with olive oil and giving them herbs such as verbena for labor pains, sometimes using warm water and sponges to relax the expectant mother. Many times their attempts were futile and the mother would die during childbirth from bleeding to death. If they survived the birth the midwife would cut the umbilical cord and take out the placenta so as to not cause infection. If the baby got stuck during the delivery sharp hooks would be used to extract the baby. If the baby was acceptable the midwife would perform a roman ritual of placing the child on the ground for the head of the household to view then claim it to rear. There was such a high mortality rate that babies were not given names for eight days for girls and nine days for boys. During the middle ages, if a baby was unwanted they could be taken to a foundling wheel that was a revolving wooden barrel lodged in a wall, often in a convent, that allowed women to deposit their offspring without being seen.

Dating back to The Iliad and The Odyssey, Homer's famous poems each divided into 24 books that follows the Greek hero Odysseus's ten year journey home following the Trojan War. Though there were female warriors such as the Amazons, most women were wives or slaves. They were objects of lust and pleasure for men and in both stories they used their sex to manipulate men. Briseis and Chryseis were girls captured during the spoils of war and used as sex slaves. Woman were seen as the deceivers and schemers with tricks up their sleeves and men were seen as the creatures filled with uncontrollable lust that fell for them. The Odyssey was filled with sirens that were half woman half bird creatures that would perch on rocks by the sea and sing beautiful songs that would lure men, who when refused to leave, would die of starvation. In his poem the nymph Calypso who is said to have held up the pillars of the sky and the sea, holds Odysseus on her island for seven years and promises him immortality and entice him by singing and playing her loom trying to make him forget about his ongoing search for his wife Penelope.

In Greek mythology women were often portrayed as temptresses consumed with evil. Lamia was known as a child-eating monster and was regarded as a night-haunting spirit. Gello was known as a female demon who threatened the reproductive cycle by causing infertility, miscarriages, and mortality. The Gorgons are famous sisters known as Stheno and Euryale and Medusa. Though not always considered evil, at one time Medusa had actually been portrayed as a beautiful priestess of the Temple of Athena, but would later be described as a winged human female with venomous snakes for hair and it was said that those that gazed at her would be turned to stone. Hekate was the goddess of magic, witchcraft, the night, the moon, ghosts, and necromancy. There was also Eris the goddess of discord, Enyo the goddess of destruction, Deimos and Phobos the goddesses of panic and terror, Apate the goddess of deceit, The Erinyes the goddess of vengeance and Moros the goddess of doom. And the list goes on and on; a whole plethora of female evil entities ready to wreak havoc on the peoples of the time, namely men.

Westward Movement and Perceptions of a New Age.....

As we move evermore towards modern times, the opening of the time capsule of the Medieval and Tudor times finds childbirth still very dangerous leaving one in three women dying during their childbearing years in the Medieval era alone. Though all aspects of motherhood and delivery are openly discussed today, it was kept a private matter back then. It did not matter your age, social status, or if you had the best care in the world, it was inevitably probable you would die during childbirth or from an infection soon afterwards.

Medicine was quite different then, and obviously not as advanced as today. There were no home pregnancy tests and often women did not even know they were pregnant until they felt the baby kicking at about five months. Unreliable tests were the only ones available during the Tutor era. A doctor would examine the color of a woman's urine and analyze its color. A lighter color was speculated to be not pregnant while a darker cloudier color signified a woman was. Another way they attempted to determine if a woman was pregnant was by leaving a needle in her urine to see if it rusted or seeing what wine mixed with her urine appeared like. Missed periods were not always a tale-tale sign because there were other factors that could have caused that like there are today. Stress, eating badly, excessive exercise can all result in missed periods.

Midwives were the women that were counted on to help with the preparation of the pregnant woman getting her ready for birth and then, when the time came, helping her birth her baby. She lacked knowledge that doctors have today but she would have been aware of what was known at the time like the best practices to use and making the best attempts of having a safe delivery. In 1513, the first birth figures were printed that were illustrated by Martin Caldenbach for Eucharius Rosslin's midwifery manual that explored and defined the pregnant body that had for centuries been shrouded in mystery and secrecy. These birth figures captivated not only commoners with a peek inside a woman's pregnant womb, but they also helped midwives envision what the position of babies were and how she might alter a babies position and physically guide labor. Rebecca Whitely theorized that for many midwives this was a newly interventionist approach that fundamentally reformulated midwifery as an active process of aid rather than a passive attendance on an inherently invisible, mysterious, and uncertain event. The illustrations gave the illusion in a microscopic rendering that the child itself was a person in the center of the universe and the encircling womb a metaphor for the sphere of the world.

Midwives were also held with suspicion in early England during a time when some were accused of witchcraft, charm, and sorcery because of their knowledge of procreation, fertility, successful delivery, and most controversial and taboo contraception and abortion. This made them vulnerable to anyone's whims of actuation of ill-willed intentions of these women who, because of their skill, were privy to personal information of the pregnant woman such as a patient who had become pregnant through an affair or sexual problems. They also had the earliest access to the babies allowing them to be accused of wrong-doing if there was a problem with the baby or death. Witches were often thought of as baby stealers and of handing them over to the devil and unfortunately midwives were sometimes perceived as evil too. They were also sometimes accused of stealing the umbilical cord and placenta to use for satanic purposes. But midwives were needed in the help and aid of pregnant women and unless you were poor living outside of cities where a family member would assist, you would most likely feel confident knowing one was at your side to assist in your birth. Most of the knowledge that midwives had was passed down from older midwives before them.

Queens and women of higher classes would isolate themselves before birth referred to as 'lying in' or 'taking her chamber' and leading up to this would be a very important service at the church with prayers to God for a successful birth wherein the Queen would then go to her chambers to wait for the birth. Most women just used a local priest to bless them before they would lay in wait for the baby to be born. The poor, just as today, were likely to have had to work right up to the time of their birth. Their birthing rooms were made to replicate the womb and were kept dark with only a small window open for fresh air. Tapestries filled the room to block off unwanted light because they feared light could hurt the expectant mother's eyes and crosses and crucifixes adorned the walls and were engraved within the tapestries. No men were allowed in the birthing rooms and it was a female lead group of women. A male physician or doctor would have only been called in in extreme emergencies like had been the case in the birth of Jane Seymore's child who had developed complications during delivery. After the English Reformation the crucifixes and Catholic relics were done away with along with the ceremonies at the church before the woman would go to her chamber.

A Queen's role was to produce an heir. Henry VIII's reign saw this become a huge issue leading to his divorce from Queen Isabella of Spain when he deemed the relationship unholy and cursed because she had been his brother's wife and he claimed was the reason she could not give him a child. Anne Boleyn also suffered the fate of not producing an heir and whether true or not, she was accused by Henry of incest with her brother that cleared the way to have her beheaded. Charles II's wife suffered several miscarriages and people within his court would push for a divorce but he always defended her honor even when rumors spread that she had tried to poison him. She eventually died without securing an heir. Queens were supposed to be virgin's at the time of marriage and many were brought to the king from other countries for political alliances and she would be expected to have a son to continue the bloodline and produce the next king. We've seen this in modern day life with Prince Charles who had to marry not for love but because he needed to produce a son for the future of the monarchy. One son was typically not considered enough either because having more than one secured the crown in the event something would happen to the first born. The pressure was ever so great to get pregnant, carry the child to term, then have a healthy baby boy.

Many wealthy women and higher society used wet nurses as a means to feed the baby but not just anybody would have been chosen to do this task. Someone was chosen based on their habits, health, and moral fortitude and temperament. Not only would they be feeding the baby but they would be his caregiver for his first years and it was believed that these years were formative years and parents wanted them to be formed by someone that they felt had high integrity to pass off desirable traits to their offspring. The family would closely monitor the wet nurse making sure their child was being taken care of properly and that she herself was taking care of her own health.

During these times childbirth was generally very painful. As the years progressed Anaesthesia was introduced in the 1850's to reduce the pain after Queen Victoria had used it during her labour. 70 years later a procedure called 'Twilight Sleep' became popularized by those who did not want to feel any pain at all during childbirth. German doctors were using it in their clinics, a drug that would do away with the pain and actually had you forgetting the entire event all together. Because American doctors found this to be too dangerous due to the drug's side effects, wealthy women were traveling across the seas to have this Twilight sleep implemented during their birth. This set off one of the first rebellions of women led by doctors and wealthier women to bring these types of clinics to America and through their determination the doctors were forced to open up maternity units in hospitals offering the drug to those who wanted it. The procedure was not all without problems and women squirmed about, soiled themselves and had to be strapped down. They probably did endure pain but they probably just forgot about it. Those days were ruled by kings and by their religion and motherhood fell in line with the times until we moved forward into even more modern times.

What Does It All Mean and Where Do We Go From Here?.....

The world as we know has been around for more than five billion years but her birth baffles us as we try and theorize different scenarios like the Big Bang Theory for science minded people and origin stories like the Biblical story of God creating the world in seven days for Christians, Mohamud as a prophet for the Muslims and The Dalai Lama's wisdom as a guide for the people of India. We started out so ornate and simple with the hunters and gatherers perceiving birth and conception much different than the feminist views of today. There were no women marching around in pink pussy hats chanting to the tune of "My body, my choice." It was Primal, side by side with the other living animals giving birth in caves and on the cold Earth floor. There weren't any love making Kamasutra manuals or, Men are from Mars, Women are from Venus type of books, life was primal coming into the world and going out. The cycle of life was pure and certain. However many of the earliest civilizations believed in an afterlife and some believed we would travel through the underworld after death only to return to our bodies here on earth at a later time. The mummification of Egyptian people and their animals is a prime example of the links they took to ensure their bodies would be intact for their future return. Female deities have been seen throughout the civilizations as the guiding forces for women to celebrate their strengths, harness their female energy and power, and demonstrate faith in feminine prowess and fertility. As we traveled through time we went through many different transformations of body and soul. Then as time went on we moved into a cycle of purity and chastity. Saving yourself for marriage became a montra and religious beliefs began to dictate our sexual attitudes. We engaged in sex to reproduce. And not that it was the first time in history but we looked for mates where we could gain prestige from the pairing. We wanted to come up in society. Women came with dowries and we were expected to take the man's last name and their union's offspring would carry on his name. Women cared for the children while the men worked and were career minded. Divorce was frowned upon and the word obey in the wedding vows was more literal than it is today. Women were certainly a second class citizen not even having the right to vote. Women were expected to be focussed on motherhood and this is the way Europe and America would be for many years. As years went by, we entered a sexual and cultural revolution in the 60's. Gone were the days where your reputation demanded you remain a virgin until marriage. Women gained the right to vote and during World War II, when men were all gone fighting the war, women went to work in factories to fill the jobs the men had left behind making the items used in war like bullets and uniforms. This was the first time a lot of these women worked outside of the house and many celebrated their new independence and never looked back after the war ended. Many women realized their self–worth and wanted to be more than just housewives. They also wanted to choose when they would get pregnant if at all. Back alley abortions were taking place in cities and some women would lose their life if conditions were dirty or unprepared. When birth control was introduced to society, women were completely in control of their fate. They would now decide if they wanted to have a stable of kids or none at all and many times there was contention between the wife and husband on whether she should stay at home having kids or if she should join the work field. Women's voices slowly got louder and louder and they were not willing to play second fiddle to the men that had once had so much power over them; husbands, bosses, and any man trying to dictate what they should or should not do with their lives and their bodies. The sixties was full of sexual freedom where one night stands and sexual exploration were applauded and not frowned upon. It has been accelerating through the 70's, 80's and now we are in a whole new sexual world where the internet plays a huge role in how sex is viewed and explored. Porn is a billion dollar industry. Tender has young teens swiping left and right for one night stands, Craigslists hosts "Any kind of sex you might be looking for '' groups and there are apps to meet and hook up with farmers, people over 50, and pretty much anybody else you might be into. Women feel that the sky's the limit now. Many aren't feeling inclined to take their husband's name, and they are waiting longer to have kids. They want to have careers and the right to choose whether they will bring a life into this world. Some claim that there are too many kids now, and they have a point. There are a lot of pitter pattering feet moving around the planet while others say that we are not reproducing enough like we did in the baby-boomer generation.

One thing is for certain, women today truly benefited from the perseverance and brevity of those who came before them. It was only 100 years ago that women were on the front lines of the Women's Suffrage Movment that had women fighting for decades for the right to vote. In 1848, Lucretia Mott and Elizabeth Cady Stanton lobbied for women to have the same rights as men by hosting the Seneca Falls Convention which was the first of its kind for women. Years later, the 19th amendment passed in 1919, and was ratified in 1920, that technically guarnted women to right to vote in the United States through women of color would still be unable to exercise this right. Now, only a short time later, we are possibly on the heels of electing the firtst femal president of color, and whether you agree with her politics or not, it is still a huge step for women who have stood in the shadows for far too long waiting to shine in the spotlight.

Natural birth, C-sections and Water Births..... The Baby's Coming Like It or Not

Me pregnant with River

Labor is hard and intensive and generally necessary in the birthing process unless you have scheduled a c-section and you bypass the pain of hours of labor. It seems like tons of mothers I talk to now have had at least one c-section. They are so much more common than they had been in the past. I feel like as soon as a doctor feels like things aren't moving fast enough you are wheeled off for a c-section. I'm sure doctors are petrified of lawsuits nowadays and don't want to take chances with a baby's life. Some women are adamant that they want their child born naturally, which means without any drugs at all. No epidural because they are gonna endure the pain and not bring a child into the world while they are under the influence of any drug. Some women just have it in them but, I on the other hand, couldn't get that epidural in me quick enough. When they would ask for a number on a scale for the amount of pain I was feeling I would double that number maybe even triple it letting them know I was ready for the epidural a half an hour after my water broke and before real labor pains had set in. So I guess my pain threshold is not that high. Some women opt to have water births that seem like a beautiful and natural way of having your baby come into the world in a soothing bathtub of water but some hospitals do not allow them because they think they are too dangerous.

Many will allow the laboring part of the delivery but once it's time for the pushing to start they require you to move to a bed. You can have a midwife assist you in your choice at home in a birthing tub or at a birthing center. But there is always a chance that something could go wrong such as infection, meconium aspiration, and drowning. There have been limited studies done on the safety of this type of delivery and more studies need to be done. In the movie pieces of a woman, Vanessa Kirby gives a stunning performance of a young mother who tries to have a home birth at home with a midwife and gets into her bathtub during the laboring part but ultimately things take a turn for the worse and help does not come soon enough to save her baby leaving her to deal with the horrible loss of her child. If she would have had the baby in the hospital, the baby probably could have been saved. It is loosely based on a true story but I'm sure there are more stories out there like this.

Some women shouldn't consider a water birth if they have gestational diabetes, preeclampsia, macrosomia, intrauterine growth restriction, prematurity, and unproven pelvis because these conditions already have you at a high-risk. Though the soothing hot water can help relieve the terrible pain of labor, like it does for menstrual cramps, it is sometimes just not worth the risks it poses. Once the baby leaves the birth canal it should be brought to the surface within ten seconds in a gentle manner to breathe the life giving oxygen it will need to survive. If things aren't done correctly the baby can suffocate. They have an inbuilt physiological reflux called the Dive reflex that prevents them from taking a breath until they're out into the open air. But in circumstances where things all run smoothly, the baby is supplied oxygen from the placenta through the umbilical cord. Some women are overwhelmingly happy with their water births believing it lessened their labor pain, kept them from tearing, and allowed the baby to be born into a welcoming atmosphere. Those opting for home births are often pleased with their outcome as well but some mothers do indeed need to be rushed to the hospital when complications do arise and sometimes the help could in fact come too late. C-sections can make births more easy because you don't have to have long drawn out labors that can last days and instead you have an appointment and go in to have the procedure done. Sometimes this option won't be utilized though until it is the last resort so you might endure hours of labor but then still need to get the c-section. Some women find this less intimate and they want to have a baby the old-fashion way and endure the labor, the dilation, the waiting game, the tearing, and the tiring period of pushing.

Everyone is different with their own wishes and desires for their delivery. Sometimes these change with second and third kids. Some women might want to have a natural birth and by the time the pain gets unbearable they scream for the epidural but the time has come and gone when it could have been administered and they have to endure the pain till the end. Women who have experience usually will opt for one on the second go around. Maybe on a woman's home birth complications occur with her first child so she wants to be absolutely sure with a future pregnancy and decides to have the baby at the hospital with a doctor or others just the opposite, finding the hospital was too stale and they want to have the baby at home. So many possibilities but in the end it's up to the woman and whether she has any additional risk factors that could jeopardize the baby's safety if she chooses a non-traditional route for delivery. One way or another, a pregnant mom's baby will need to be born, and the mom has many months sitting around her home to decide how she'll have it. In the end, there is no pain-free way to give birth but the reward is your little bundle of joy.

My story: The good, The Bad, and The Ugly.......

So my story began as a second child born to a Mom and Dad married into the suburban dream of owning a house in the suburbs, the dream of so many of the time. My mom was a virgin who religiously waited to have sex until marriage and like popcorn started popping my brothers and I out one by one so that by 23 or so she had three small toddlers running around going crazy. I was a confident child and was always eager to be included in my brother's high jinks and male-based life of sports, wrestling, Etc. If I got a baby doll for Christmas or a Barbie baby carriage my brothers would laugh hysterically upon the unwrapping of the gift while I hysterically cried. From a small age I wanted no part of it, this "Baby thing." One baby doll I got peed and had diapers and I was completely not amused by my toy expecting me to clean up its mess. I was so envious watching my brothers open gifts like Stretch Armstrong and magic trick compilation boxes and would loathe them while watching them play with their fun new gifts while the pee doll sat in the corner staring at me as if to say, "Hey over here, I need a diaper change." And then when

I was in third grade my dad left because my mom found out he was seeing someone else and that's when my life took a massive turn in a different direction or more like a swerve into a tree on the side of the road. I lost interest in school that I had excelled in, became emotional, depressed, and suicidal. I watched my family fall apart and my mom was left to pick up the broken pieces. I became a latchkey kid so she could go to work during the day and law school at night. So where I had once had a stay at home doting Mom making school lunches, sowing Halloween costumes and helping us create our winning science projects, now I was left to fend for myself. There wasn't a lot of money so I was envious of friends who got the latest fashionable clothes, had a lot of food being cooked for them three times a day and had a nice house. I hated our house, hated having to get the new generic brand food that was just introduced to the needy while my dad was driving around with his girlfriend in a Corvette going on trips and hanging out in chic bars while we sat at home with broken promises of him picking us up for a weekend, but even when he did decide to show up, it almost made it seem worse. I would become fully aware of the stark contrast seeing his nice clean air conditioner apartment compared to our blazing hot dirty house and it made me even more bitter. We had been abandoned in the disgusting suburbs like some discarded feral animals that had once been cute little house pets, but we weren't the only ones, because almost every other house on our street had the same scene playing out as if everybody had received the same script. The scenes of paint beginning to chip, grass growing a little higher, and mom's trying desperately to cling to one another to try and recoup their pride going out for a Friday night coming back a little worse off than the way they had left. Like the movie 9 to 5 with a glimpse of The Exorcist, our lives were weird and, though other kids might have had it harder, through a kid's eyes, it felt like this was our dismal existence and ours alone. The mothers would call each other in tears to console each other because all of us kids were totally out of control. My older brother stole money from my mom's purse, another was arrested for shoplifting but I was by far the worst. I spray painted part of the outside of the house days after it was painted ignoring the fact my mom had saved money for a long while to have it done. I was doing drugs, skipping school, drinking til I was blacked out, even getting arrested for driving drunk the first night I got my license. A real mess. My mom did the best she could but there were many days and nights she laid in bed crying defeated and I saw the same picture in every window on every house on our block. My reaction was in sync with many I knew going through the same thing. I spent hours sitting on this little board at the top of my closet painting devils, cutting myself, ditching school and getting as wasted as as often as I could while a serial murder who was known as "The East Area Rapist" was roaming our streets tormenting wives and husbands and I was left home by myself in fear our house would be the next one hit. One night I layed in bed and was awakened by big flashing lights coming through my bedroom window and loudspeakers started shouting "He's in the backyard," from the helicopters above. I awoke in terror, sweating profusely because only my younger brother had been home and I was sure whoever was in the backyard was ready to smash the window in and attack me. The mayhem lasted for a few minutes until the helicopter's propellers slowly faded off into the distance leaving me by myself laying in my bed frozen not knowing if he was left behind in my backyard. On another hot Sacramento night my mom had left her bedroom window open to cool down her bedroom because we didn't have air conditioning and some days would get to be close to 110 degrees and I would have to take a cold shower every hour or so just to cool off. But on this night, she went to close the window that I often begged her not to leave open and as she was winding the window crank to close it she saw two pair of eyes peering back at her from a crouched position. She screamed and the would-be intruder or rapist scurried off into the dark night.

There were no lines men were afraid to cross while in authority. Numerous bosses would display inappropriate behavior at my places of employment, one even asking me if I wanted to go into the backroom with him and lay down and take a break. The dean of my school who was later arrested and put in prison for sleeping with some of the girls at the school, came to my house asking why I wasn't ever at school then proceeded to ask me for a hug while pressing his body against mine in my dimly lit living room. He had known what type of girls to go after because they were all the ones from broken homes or ones like me who had been seeing the school psychologist. But I wasn't interested in him, moreover, I just wanted to keep him off my back from cutting school so he ended up going to get a lighter outta his car for me so I could light my cigarette. Everyday after that I would see him in the school halls asking kids where I was like some stalker from the internet. It didn't matter though because I spent more time outta school partying than I did in school studying.

These times had me going straight to that cupboard that all the same latchkey kids families had in their homes, those liquor cupboards stocked for entertaining, and over time I emptied every single one of them and replaced them with water. It's a good thing my mom never got in there cuz her drinks would have been non-alcoholic without her knowing it. She did the best she could and ended up ranking top of her class in law school, passing the Bar Exam on her first try, and managing to raise three kids on her own so I would consider hers, "A success story." And it's not just a success story because she passed but it's because of the adversity that she had to face predating this feat. When she grew up she had been dirt poor. She had to donate blood just to have money to eat. Sometimes they, her mom and her, would have to sleep in the car by the airport or wherever else they could find an out of the way spot. At one point she had to live in an orphanage because her mom simply could not care for her or her brothers and sisters. Food was so scarce sometimes they would mix sugar with water and that would be their meal. She never was able to go to college so she took a special test to bypass that process and was able to enroll directly into a law school. At that time there were far fewer women enrolling but she was dedicated and determined to do well. She would wake up at the crack of dawn and go to work downtown as a secretary then it was off to law school at night and weekends were for focussing on studying and going to the grocery store and doing other chores that the weekdays had not allowed and she somehow managed to get by on a shoe-string budget. That's why when she took the bar exam we were in a state of anxiety as a family to find out the results because, if she passed, we knew that she would have little extra money to buy new clothes, more food, and the small things in life that makes one feel good about themselves. I remember coming home from school one day and there it was a big piece of paper taped to the front door that said "I PASSED," and I ran into the house screaming, jumping up and down with my mom, ecstatic that all of her hard work had paid off and the struggles that all of us had endured while she was always away from the house at work and school, had not been in vain and we opportunistically turned our sights to a brighter future.

My mom in court

My mom in my grand father's pool

I spent years partying, never finishing things I started. I had two abortions but I didn't feel guilty at all. I just knew I didn't want to have a kid and, though there were precautions I could've taken, I was too irresponsible. I couldn't even keep track of my own purse when I was drunk let alone remember to take a daily pill. My mom was a staunch Catholic that had been a volunteer in one of those anti-abortion groups and I think I remember her even having a fetus in a jar one time but I'm not sure but she would have been mortified by my decisions. I think the other was an ectopic pregnancy. I had been on a bender drinking out at some club with my then boyfriend and his friends and at some point they found me huddled over in pain and I might have passed out and was rushed to the hospital. Turns out I was like three or four months pregnant but it was growing in my tube so it needed to be terminated and they said it could have killed me.

Not until I joined an all girl punk band with three other girls at a time when most girls were supposed to be the groupies not the ones playing the music but somehow we managed to become a really good band and people loved us and we toured in the US and Europe drinking our way across the states. I still had no desire whatsoever to have a kid. In fact, I was the one in the band that said I never wanted kids but one day that changed. I saw some kids playing at the school in front of my house and I was like "I wonder if I should have a kid?"

I was 27 at the time and by the time I was 28 I was giving birth to my first boy Lane. Not an easy birth because I ended up having to get a c-section, a procedure that has you getting your stomach sliced open while you're still awake. Yea, pretty brutal for modern times but still better than days past that most likely would have meant a sure death for me. I was in so much pain afterward in the hospital that every time I moved there was a horrendous feeling like being stabbed. And if I laughed, it was even worse. Someone had a Tickle me Elmo doll in the hallway one night, probably one of my baby gifts, and I remember the doll laughing like they do and for some reason I thought it was the funniest thing ever and started laughing while pain spread out from my stomach like an exploding nuclear bomb causing me to buckle, but the more I tried not to laugh, the funnier it became. So basically I was torturing myself with my own laughter and the juxtaposition of the pain and the laughter was an odd fate lying in that hospital bed by myself. But my son was not one of those types of kids to sit silently in the corner sucking his thumb. He was ready to put the pedal to the metal at all times and it was a lot to deal with for someone who had recently been touring and partying every night. I was not ready to have to have someone need me 24/7 and at that time, though I wasn't a horrible person or mom, I just wasn't great either. His dad and I were both dysfunctional people from dysfunctional homes so trying to play house was messy and unpredictable. He had mommy issues and I had daddy issues so we were on a collision course that was doomed from the start with deep-seated resentments for the opposite sex. By the time we had our second son things were headed in a horrible direction and addiction had taken control until he ended up in rehab and I was on my own with the two boys. I found myself in some bizarre place in my life like if you've ever been driving down the street singing along to that Meatloaf song "And I would do anything for love, but I won't do that?" and after like two or three seconds you're thunderstruck by a lightning bolt and think to yourself, "What the hell is THAT?"

All of a sudden I was completely in charge of a house, bills, kids, a job, and anything that entails the definition of the word "responsible." The person who had been fucked up her whole life was now in charge of everything. I started dating someone who my son knew who was a lot younger than me but everyone was just hanging out and I hung out with all young people and to this day a lot of people seem to be affected by the age difference that I've never witnessed when the tables are turned and the man's older than the woman. In fact, some people seem irritated by it, the age difference which is mind-boggling to me because every person I see judging me I could pick them apart with a list of their 'not so savory' past and present choices. I was not your typical mom type. I had been on tour pregnant not that long before this, I was playing in bands up to about this point and I was never one to follow rules or follow any mantra. However, this was not the best decision because my son got pissed but by this time it was too late because we were hanging out every day. I was not a typical mother in that I was hanging out at skateparks, smoking cigarettes, and not conforming to society and its rules. I was never gonna be a sheep following everyone around and that was how I was from day one and why I got into punk in the first place. I was a verifiable misfit with emotional problems but now it was time for me to get my shit together. While some people's biggest accomplishments are getting jobs and climbing the company ladder or graduating with a 4.0, in my mind mine was getting to play the iconic CBGB'S club in New york City before it closed down that saw the likes of the Ramones, Blondie, and The New York Dolls gracing it's stage.

Around this time I got pregnant and had a date to have an abortion but the dad begged me not to and, though I knew this was gonna be an uphill battle, I decided to cancel the appointment and was eventually blessed with a girl we named River. In retrospect, I'm so happy that I changed my mind because otherwise she wouldn't be here today and I would've missed out on the blessing in my life. It's surreal to think that she wouldn't have been here if I would have gone to that appointment that day. But almost 14 years later her dad and I are still together, we got married, and though things aren't perfect, I would say we get along good and have hung out almost everyday for all those years. I dont trip on the age difference. I'm always ready to GO and am the one that planned trips around the world, skydiving, rafting down the Grand Canyon and I haven't fallen yet and yelled out "I can't get up." All the years since the boys and I's dad and I split up, I've had to deal with taking kids to hospitals, doctors, braces, attitudes, school clothes, groceries, police, arrests, and what feels like endless school meetings with groups of teachers staring at me telling me how my kid is outta control and failing while I pretended to be something that I'm not cordially agreeing when I had been the worst student ever. I would say "Ok great! let's implement whatever plan you have" and then walk outta the school thinking "Whew! That's over with" thinking that the future was looking bright until the next day when I would get the call from the same teachers because my kid hadn't shown up to school so it was back to the drawing board and back to the center of the circle of teachers and principals staring at me.

"So are kids a good idea? Is motherhood all it's cracked up to be?" Well, for me they somewhat saved me because I came to realize it wasn't all about me and all the self-pity I had had disappeared. At least there was a real attempt now to not be a total fuck up. I was present and tried to take them places to teach them about the world by actually becoming a part of other cultures and visiting other geographies. I was never a mom that was a disciplinarian so I got an F in that category but I tried the best I could. Having a daughter is a whole nother ball game. I have a lotta friends that have told me that they were molested as young kids. I never had that happen to me when I was really young so it's something I try to protect her from at all costs. Though I know the perpetrator can be a female, most of the time they're male so I do my best to make sure she's not around any males by herself and though that sounds messed up, I would never want her coming to me telling me stories like the ones my friends told me. All the years of being selfish, a complete drunk, someone who lasted at a job for no more than a few months before just not showing up after a night partying, now I was a responsible employee clocking into my same job everyday 23 years later.

For me I don't regret the abortions I had though I believe they are just that. Aborting a kid is killing a kid and there's no way around that but in retrospect, I don't know if I would still do it especially after my daughter River but that's because I love her dad. If it was with someone I didn't like I don't know and luckily for me I won't have to make that decision again. I have a wavering opinion because I think children and beautiful creatures are kinda what it seems like it's all about. I was born a baby and now am older and it's a cyclical cycle that cycles through birth to death and the process seems natural to me.

But I wouldn't want to make that decision for someone else and I also see the position through the eyes of those who are opposed to it.

There have been a lot of lessons learned throughout my time as a mother with kids that range from 26 all the way down to 8. Lessons I don't think that I would have learned otherwise. I walk with two steps forward everyday walking into the unknown and spend little time looking back. I don't ever sit around feeling sorry for myself or hating myself for anything from my past. If I'm still breathing, that's simply another day to try and do better.

My dad ended up going from being a lawyer to a homeless person on the street because he didn't want to work and I watched him deteriorate over the last years of his life. He would show up at my house uninvited and sometimes I would wake up to him coughing outside my window smoking a cigarette with the smoke billowing up into my room and always on a night where the next day I would have something important going on. I would eventually let him in and he would have all his smelly clothes and blankets with him and my OCD would kick into overdrive. By now he looked terrible and his teeth were falling out and he was smoking like a pack of cigarettes a day. I would sit down with him exhausted and go over a life plan writing down phone numbers of shelters, jobs, etc. that could get him on the right track but I knew as soon as he left my house it would be right back to the same old thing which was a whole lotta nothing. When he was at my house he was too lazy to go up the stairs to use the bathroom and would just pee off my porch in front. I had spent so many years crying about him and now I had become like his mom but I had no more tears left for him. I realized everyone is on there own path in life and this was his and I got a call one day that he had collapsed walking down the street and died and that was the end of his story and, sad to say I guess, but not one tear was shed from my oldest brother who had also unsuccessfully tried to help him or myself. So who knows maybe he will return here on earth someday to learn lessons that were not learned in this lifetime and maybe I will too. But for now I try to live one day at a time doing the best I can.

Abortion For What It's Worth and Birth Control's History.....

This topic is as hot as a scalding kettle, as current as today's news and as debated as a topic on a college debating team so one must tread lightly when discussing it because it encompasses so many different emotions and moral and social ideas and beliefs. People are passionate about it and some even aggressive going to Planned Parenthood sites and igniting bombs outside their doors. Others have marched up and down city streets carrying signs of "My body my Choice" and using violence at the rally's if needed to get their point across. Feelings run deep about the matter. I honestly would not want to be a Supreme Court judge voting on the matter because I understand everyone's point of view and there is validity to both sides of the argument, but if I were, I would vote in favor of it because otherwise women would be backed into a dangerous corner. But, the issue is in the forefront of politics now and has people more engaged than ever before so I guess I should just start from the beginning. From the beginning of civilizations people have practiced birth control using herbs and remedies to try and stop the conception of a child and babies have been killed throughout history for different reasons such as sacrifices and deformities of the fetus. Throughout history there have been different views on the subject and in the past there wasn't always a stigma around birth control. Coming into more recent times the church and politicians have made it more of a moral issue that has pushed the topic to the forefront. It was well documented in Egyptian times with the Egyptians using honey, acadia leaves, and lent as a way to block the sperm. In the first Egyptian medical text, The Kahun Gynecological Papyrus, there was evidence that they used acacia gum that has proven to have spermatocyte qualities that are still used in contraceptive jellies today. Some women of the time opted to breastfeed for up to three years to prevent pregnancy right after the birth of a child.

In ancient Greece and the ancient East, they too looked for ways to prevent an unwanted child again using plants such as Silphium that is a giant Fennel and a related species Asafoetida that would be used as an oral contraceptive. So many different plants and herbs have been used throughout time, some efficiently, while others were no more than an old wive's tale. You would be playing Russian roulette when trying to use these methods, sometimes staying safe while other times becoming pregnant.

Other plants used at this time were willow, date palm, pomegranate, artemisia, rue and Queen Anne's lace that is still used today in India.

Some methods were outright dangerous with women who didn't want kids encouraged to drink a concoction of copper salt that was promised to prevent pregnancy for a year but that in many instances would lead to fatality. Many people were trying to come up with ways to prevent conception. Even Aristotle had put his two cents in by claiming that cedar oil was effective in preventing pregnancy.

China and India also had ways to try and prevent pregnancy. dating back as far as the Tang Dynasty, they would prescribe oil and quicksilver that would have been heated together for an entire day then taken orally for sterility. In India, they used coitus obstructs that involves controlling the release of semen. In the Ancient Americas, the Hopi and Tewa used Indian paintbrush as one method of contraceptive while the Navahos and Shoshoni used Lithosperum. Different tribes used different plants to try and achieve sterility or prevention such as Prunus emarginata, veratrum caliorniicum, and maianthemum stellatum. People of the time just tried anything in their environment that they thought might work and at these more primitive times, they were not aware of the rhythem method and did not have means of modern day birth control.

The Persians too tried to prevent unwanted babies even using elephant dung, cabbage, and pitch to block a female's cervix. Rock salt was used as well. Religion came into play in these earlier times when Mohammud, the Muslim Prophet, opposed these prevented measures. He would not be the only one because in Europe during the medieval times it was considered immoral to try and prevent pregnancy by the Catholic Church even though you would be chastised and sent away if you were an unwed mother. Though these times had people scrutinized harshly, some still used Lily root and rue, inserting it into their vaginas to block the sperm from traveling to the egg.

In South Asia, they used potions made of powdered palm leaf and seeds of the palasa tree, ghee, honey and red chalk. Every single tribe, civilization, and people looked for ways to control their own destiny. Women had different reasons for not wanting to become pregnant. Unwed mothers, families without the means to care for more children, those who had sex outside of the marriage, there have always been reasons someone would not want to have a child. But many times the attempts made to not become pregnant were in vain and a woman would find herself bearing a child anyway. And before abortion became a medical procedure, infamticide would be implemented to do away with a baby. Many times the baby would simply be left to the elements where they would die from the cold or starvation. Other times they would be killed by being smothered or some other cold way that would leave the parents free of the unwanted child. If the baby was deformed he would many times be harshly scrutinized then killed. The attitudes of the time are much different than they are today with this practice being considered barbaric and illegal.

Coming into more modern times attitudes slowly changed and are still crisscrossing across the pentalum of what should be legal and illegal. It's been an ever evolving conversation with many different people throwing their opinions into the ring. In Britain in 1778, a man named Thomas Maltus argued in an essay on the Principle of Population, that population grows in times of plenty until it has stripped away all of its resources. He claimed that there were positive checks such as the raising of the death rate by hunger, disease and war, while there were preventative checks such as abortion, birth control, prostitution, postponement of marriage and celibacy. His views held the opinion that the populations were held within their own resource limits.

Men were not the only ones with opinions about a woman's reproductivity and women's voices were becoming louder as well. They coined the phrase "voluntary motherhood" in 1870 which implied that women had the right to reject unwanted sex and could choose if and when they had children. The opponents to this argued that women should only engage in sex to procreate or remain abstinent. As the timeline moved forward, Victorian women had become educated about the issues and were able to utilize condoms and diaphragms.

Margarat Sanger opened a short-lived birth control clinic in 1916 that would be shut down only nine days later. This prompted activists to come together and the first birth control league formed in America in 1921. This league was responsible for the openings of birth control clinics and education of women to control their own fertility. Marie Stopes wrote a very popular book of the times called Married Love that focussed on ways to have a successful marriage and discussed birth control methods that, in 1918, was pretty controversial for the conservative mindset. In the past, these topics had not been spoken about so openly.

As time progressed the ideas were talked about in medical terms all across the globe making it more acceptable and less taboo, opening the way in 1921 for the first birth control clinic to be established in Mumbai. Women were being greater advocates for themselves in every way imaginable. From the thirties all the way up to the sixties and seventies, they were advocating for legislation that would ensure their access to birth control, contraceptives, and abortion rights, depending on what was available and in front of them at the time.

Gregory Pincus and John Rock, through the Planned Parenthood Federation of America, developed the first birth control pills in the 50's that were more widely distributed during the sixties. Medical abortion in the 1970's used a class of drugs to terminate pregnancies using Prostaglandin analogs and in the 1980's Mifepristone was used that was 97 percent effective in terminating a pregnancy in the first 63 days of pregnancy.

Laws were being developed along the way concerning all of these issues. In 1965 the Supreme Court ruled in the case of *Griswold vs. Connecticut* in a landmark decision that protected the liberty of married couples to buy and use contraceptives without government restrictions. In 1972 in the *Eisenstadt vs. Baird* case ruled and established the right of unmarried people to possess contraception on the same basis as married couples. In 1967 the *Neuwirth Law* was implemented in France that lifted the ban on birth control methods and the *Veil Act* was resurrected in 1975 legalizing abortion. One of the most famous decisions was made in 1973 in the *Roe vs. Wade* case that ruled that the constitution of the United States protected a pregnant woman's individual liberty to have an abortion, but in June of 2022, this law was overturned in the ruling of *Dobbs vs.*

Jackson Women's Health Organization, that had challenged a ban of abortion that was 15 weeks into the pregnancy thus ending the federal constitutions rights to abortion in the United States of America.

Planned Parenthood, which has played a major part in the education of reproductive rights claims that one in three women living in states where abortion is no longer accessible because, months after *Roe vs. Wade* was overturned, 18 states banned or severely restricted abortion. As I write, even more states are working on it. They go on to say that the Black, Latino, and Indigenous communities of color face systemic racism and have long been blocked from access to opportunity and health care.

It is believed by some activists that throughout the 1700 and 1800's herbs and medicines were used as abortion inducing methods and that it wasn't until the late 1800's where we have seen the desire to outlaw abortion in US politics. This debate is as current today with a Texas judge Kacsmaryk having recently made a preliminary injunction on a case regarding Mifepriston, a two-step abortion pill, that is used in one half of abortions today. Proponents wanted it removed from shelves until a permanent ruling was made that would ultimately be decided by the Supreme Court. People in favor of the drug unsuccessfully argued that they shouldn't be able to remove a drug that has safely been used for twenty years and this would be an unprecedented action by removing it from shelves.

Today 68.8 million US women do not have access to abortion that are of reproductive age in states where it is illegal. In 2020, it was estimated that from 700,000 to 900,000 women participated in medical induced abortions. These statistics show that women are engaged in the practice of abortion and are not opposed to terminating a pregnancy. There is a whole nother faction of people that believe that these practices are killing a baby and the debate continues around when a life truly begins. For religious reasons or for just basic reasons, some people oppose the killing of another human being to the core of their being. And those who favor it are appalled at someone trying to govern what they do with their body. The chance of these two opposing sides uniting on any front is most likely never gonna happen. That leaves it up to the courts and why the Presidency has held such an importance in the last few years, especially when he would be appointing new Supreme Court judges that would be making decisions on this contentious issue. For some, this is the utmost most important political issue while others are passionate about other issues on the ballots.

I don't know what the future holds for women and the issues surrounding fertility. It is a very personal issue, but at the same time, it involves politicians, church institutions, and families. Everyone has an opinion on the matter. If we do away with abortion all together, I fear the dreadful results because women will be left with no choice and use unsafe means to terminate the pregnancy. Some believe that there should be a deadline as to when one can access an abortion believing that it should not be allowed in the second and third trimester. Some believe that it should be allowed for rape victims and women carrying deformed or unhealthy babies while others don't even feel that that is justification enough for the procedure. I think that most would argue that no woman carrying a fetus that is unhealthy and that will die or a woman that has been raped should have to carry that child to term but the other areas are grey with many differing opinions about when the time should be "too late" in the pregnancy for the procedure. I hope a pill is invented that you can take maybe once a year to prevent pregnancy that's easy and less time consuming than condoms, creams, and diaphragms. If we spend more resources on education for prevention then less people will need access to abortion clinics. For now the debate will rage on and people will jump to their side of the aisle and only time will tell what lies ahead for women and their reproductive systems.

Miscarriage and Stillborns....
The Great Disappointment

Women across the globe have found themselves expecting a baby and some are ecstatic about the revelation. Some women plan the pregnancy while others are unexpected. Those that have planned their pregnancy have quite often waited a long time for the day to come where they found themselves carrying a child. Other women who were not planning to become pregnant are often pleasantly surprised or they slowly adapt to the news over time and start counting down the days until their child arrives in the world. Most women spend months decorating their future arrivals room choosing the perfect crib and nursing chair. When they find out the sex of the child color schemes are decided and paint is applied to the nursery walls and gender reveal parties are planned. They choose mobiles that hang from the cribs deciding from hundreds of different styles on online shopping sites. They start looking through baby naming books to try and find the perfect name. They have baby showers receiving the tiniest socks and onesies. They dream of the day they will hold their babies only for one day seeing them off to kindergarten, standing at their high-school graduation and ultimately helping them plan their weddings. But once in a while, in the flash of an eye, their dreams are stripped from them and sometimes even happening before all the real preparations begin. Other times it happens at the finish line and the baby is stillborn. Either way there is a huge loss and oftentimes a void is left behind.

Miscarriages can leave women broken. They get their hearts set on having their baby when they find out their pregnant and then one fateful day they find out they're spotting pink, red or brownish blood that is usually accompanied by cramps and pain in the lower abdomen and then the passing of tissue or blood clots from their vagina often in the toilet that render their pregnancy spontaneously terminated. Most women are shocked and have a hard time coming to terms with their sudden loss. Many feel guilty like they could have been at fault for the outcome of their little one and many women have more than one miscarriage, some even experiencing multiple of them in a row leaving the women to want to quit and just give up because they do not want to go through the tragic event again. Most miscarriages happen during the first trimester of pregnancy that is the first 12 weeks. Anytime after 20 weeks it is referred to as a stillbirth. Some women lose their child during the birthing process and the baby will be dead when born. Any stage of the loss, is still a loss because, a baby that once thrived and retained its mom's nutrients, is now no longer with them.

Most miscarriages are caused by conditions that women have no control over. Accounting for more than half of all miscarriages are chromosomal abnormalities. When fertilized eggs have too many or too few chromosomes it could either prevent the embryo from developing or from forming in the first place. Food poison can also cause you to miscarry if you become infected with listeriosis and there are lists of foods to avoid during pregnancy to avoid this. STD's can also be the culprit and you should get tested when you find out you're pregnant because many times women do not even know they have them. Scar tissue in your uterus or cervix can cause you to lose your child that can be caused by endometriosis, pelvic inflammatory disease, and cervical insufficiency. Age is a factor and after 35 you are more at risk because there is a greater chance for extra or missing chromosomes. Conditions in work environments can leave you vulnerable if you're exposed to radiation or toxic contaminants that could also be found in one's home. Smoking, drinking, and taking drugs can be factors as well as health conditions like thyroid disorders, autoimmune disorders and being over or underweight. If you have had a miscarriage in the past your chances are increased to have a repeat event.

People need to be educated though, because there are some activities like sex and physical activity that don't actually play into the causes for a miscarriage but the jury is still out on other factors like caffeine and high stress. The best thing you can do for yourself is eliminate all stress in your life as best as you can during your pregnancy, eat healthy and follow your doctor's orders. If you've had a previous miscarriage's, you might be instructed to go on bedrest until the baby is born just to be on the safeside. Sometimes it's just the way that it goes and, even when you've done everything right, you might still lose your child yet there is in fact hope because many times women go on to have many children after a miscarriage.

A stillborn baby is usually considered to be any baby that is dead before birth. There are different stages defined and an early stillbirth is when the fetus is between 20 and 27 weeks, a late stillbirth is a death occurring between 28 and 36 weeks, and even more devastating a term stillbirth occurring 37 weeks and on. Any stage can be unbearable because women are given the news that they are carrying a dead baby and they are fully aware that this means they will now be delivering their dead baby. This has to be a nightmare for all mothers. They become fully aware that they will need medical intervention to deliver the baby but nothing a doctor could do at this point could resurrect the baby's life.

The most telling sign that a woman's baby is dead is when she stops feeling movement of the child in her belly. She doesn't have those moments in the day of feeling her little one kicking and turning in utero and intuition tells her something is off. This might be accompanied by bleeding, cramping, and/or pain. This occurrence is uncommon though only occurring in about 1 percent of all pregnancies in the United states which comes to about 24,000 women having a stillbirth baby a year. But still, 24,000 women will have the burden of carrying their now dead child. Causes for this phenomenon range from infections of the fetus, mother or placenta to problems with the placenta itself such as insufficient blood flow. Certain birth defects or chromosomal abnormalities of the fetus can be the cause as well as high blood pressure of the mother. Complications of pregnancy and labor can cause a late term stillborn manifested by preterm labor or the separation of the placenta from the uterine wall. There are different reasons for these conditions to occur like obesity,

Diabetes, high blood-pressure, multiple pregnancies, and if you are under 20 or over 35. If you are African-american your chances increase, as well as, if you smoke, drink, use alcohol, or have had stillbirths or miscarriages in the past, statistics show that you are at greater odds to experience a stillbirth.

Depending on the stage of your pregnancy may determine how the baby is delivered. It might be that they decide to induce labor or a c-section might need to be performed. In any case, the dead baby must be removed from the womb and the mom will be left with intense grief. The good news is that only about 1 in 100 women will have another stillborn baby, leaving great hope for women experiencing stillbirths that they will very likely go on to have healthy babies in the future.

Like miscarriage, sometimes there is nothing you can do to prevent losing your baby because your body just can not handle it. There are ways in aiding to the health of yourself and your baby by doing everything you can to make your odds greater for a healthy child such as not smoking, drinking, taking drugs, eliminating stress and going to prenatal checkups to have ultrasounds and having a doctor keeping an eye on your babies health. Everything in life comes with risks so sometimes you have to throw caution to the wind and try to become pregnant and have a baby even if you've miscarried in the past or had a stillbirth. And sometimes after having gone through misery you will come out the other side and find yourself holding a bundle of joy.

Losing A Child When We Aren't Suppose To Die Before Our Kids....

With so much dissension in the world right now I think we can at least agree on the fact that losing a child has to be one of the worst and most painful experiences on earth. A child is expected to outlive his or her parents and although it seems like a given, sometimes tragedy strikes and the world doles out an unexpected and harsh outcome. Medicine has brought us to a place where there are much fewer deaths of babies and mothers during the birthing process with c-sections becoming a common procedure when the mother is failing to dilate over a safe time period after her water breaks, but sometimes these go awry as well. I don't know if epidurals slow down the dilation process but it happened to me with all three of my kids. I was rushed into surgery with my second kid because when they did administer the epidural it was administered wrong and I went unconscious and cords and machines were ripped out or turned off while a team of nurses and doctors rushed me out of the room and wheeled me down the hall while I was losing vitals. So abrupt and unexpected, their dad who had been sitting in the room with headphones on had not even realized for a minute or two what was going on. When he did realize he went into panic mode and rushed down the hall behind the chaos. Having been a punk rocker, for lack of a better term, all his life, when he saw a room with doctor attire he had no problem going against hospital policy and started putting on the scrubs and mask. He ran to the room I was in and the anesthesiologist was telling the other doctors that he had put the needle too far in my spinal column and I was losing all vitals and the baby. I guess when he walked into the room with the gloves the nurse assumed he was a doctor and signaled to the sanitized gloves in her hands but since he had held up his hands wrong she realized he wasn't the doctor. He said at that time I was puking up some white stuff and after some tense minutes they got the situation back under control. There will always be risk though with any type of birth whether it be natural, in water, or coincided with the use of pain drugs.

Drugs and alcohol are plaguing our communities like never before. Street drugs are being laced with Fentinal and hundreds of people are dying every day. It's in cocaine, speed pills, heroin, and is causing people to die in unprecedented numbers because only the smallest amount is needed to take someone's life. People are suffering like never before and all the money that is being thrown at the problem has only been in vain because the problem has escalated to somewhat pandemic levels. I believe that people are feeling more lonely and isolated than ever before with the internet's hold on people and possibly the loss of community through fewer spiritual gatherings or connections in personal ways other than texts or comments on a post and mental health issues are not being treated effectively.

Children are also dying from participating in stupid TIk-Tok challenges. Nylah Anderson died at age 10 trying a viral choking challenge a few years ago by attempting a black out challenge where kids hold their breath. The pressure to conform is at an all time high and people are attempting challenges on the platform that are irrational and unnecessary. Another child succumbed to the same fate attempting the challenge by tying a shoelace around his neck. In all fairness, kids with or without the internet will find ways to push the boundaries and do stupid things on whims or dares. I know this because my friends and I before the birth of the internet used to choke each other out till we passed out just to get the high from it and because we were stupid. But, I believe these platforms are pushing kids more increasingly to the extremes by enticing them to want to become famous for a day desperate for attention witnessing others gaining attention through these means.

The online bullying is at all an all time high and I have fell victim to this myself but children are fragile and sometimes they cave to it and commit suicide or go on mass shootings at schools killing innocent kids. When you get people in a pack mentality they lose their moral compass. Grown adults as well as kids are sucked into the world of online bullying hiding behind computers and posts attacking people who may not or may not even be on the platforms themselves stalking them and trolling them like teenagers. They teach their own kids everyday about not bullying anyone at school and then while their kids are at school they sit on the internet sipping their tea bullying and trolling away. When people spend all of their energy focussed on another person, where they will stop at nothing to be cruel, it becomes a real sickness within society. All the trolls, who, if they just took a good look at themselves and their own families, would realize that they would not fare so well under the spotlight of judgment. I watched a special on Tv the other day about Aaron Carter who had been a child star who's fame had faded and family issues had haunted him and he was being bullied daily on the internet by trolls who wanted to tear him apart like a piece of meat. All he wanted was their love and admiration and although they had once held him on a pedestal, now they were in a feeding frenzy to tear him apart. It was so sad watching him spiral down on drugs on the internet where he likely died in real time huffing on drugs to get high. He seemed to be someone that just wanted love but unfortunately ended up succumbing to the bullying like many do. Half the people that wanted to chastise him probably are addicts themselves or have them within their families. Trolls are able to stay relevant by being mean to other people when they themselves are far from perfect human beings many with numerous failed marriages, affairs, cheating, racism, drug addictions, and cyberbullying careers that leaves you scratching your head because when people are truly happy with themselves and their lives, they don't crave the need to try and destroy other people. There have been many teenagers that have died by suicide at the hands of people who don't care enough about humanity to curb their own thirst for attention and notoriety and when it's adressed they double-down. So many ways children see untimely deaths and Aaron Carter died prematurely and those that bullied him have probably moved on to new targets to troll night and day.

Science has brought us to a place where we are curing once incurable diseases and really working hard at finding cures for childhood cancers with St.

Judes Hospital leading the way with groundbreaking technologies. Life is filled with so many obstacles that kids sometimes succumb to, whether by choice or not, their untimely deaths. Drunk driving causes thousands of deaths a year and teenages are in that high risk category and it is why their insurance premiums are sky high. Texting while driving has disastrous results as well adding to the number of car crashes each year.

Sadly, there is no fail safe way to keep your children 100 percent safe at all times. Sometimes even when you do everything you can to help them, kids sometimes do all the things that we teach them not to do. Even straight A kids sometimes end up addicted to drugs. Mental health issues are probably at an all time high.

There is no guarantee babies won't be born with some life threatening disease or take a wrong turn in the road so I guess the takeaway is that life is fragile and at times unforgiving.

There is a chance your child could die before you and this is something that might be unavoidable and I guess the only power you have is in how you deal with the loss afterward. Everyone has different ways of coping and grieving and some find solitude in faith while others might take very dark paths. In the end, as most of us would believe, they will be reunited with their loved one in the afterlife.

Jasmin Hershberger....on the loss of her child

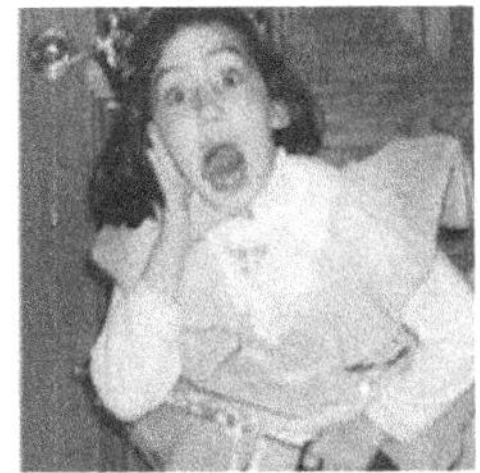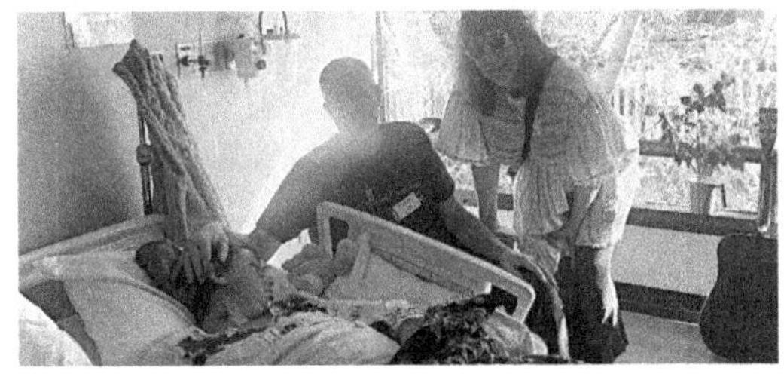

Elyssia when she ws young.
Elyssia in the hopital with Jasmin

Jasmin is someone I've known for years. She is a fellow musician but in all fairness, I'm not sure if I would qualify in that category anymore. I don't even own a guitar other than singing along to the radio that is the closest I get to music nowadays. However she was the queen of blues and I liked fast dirty, "Junkee music," but a musicians a musician, generally moody, a bit out there, and usually not inclined to the 9 to 5. I remember her and I sitting in my living room one time sitting in these rolling chairs on top of the hardwood floor and we were drinking a bottle of champaign trying to sing Janis Joplin's Bobby Mcgee but everytime we would start singing we would start laughing so hard I think one of us fell outta our chairs. We had been recording ourselves on one of those old school tape recorders and I used to replay that tape years later and it would always make me laugh listening to us trying to get through just the first line of that song.

She had two daughters when she was relatively young and did what she needed to do to get by for the next 20 years to carry them into adulthood. Both girls were raised by the same dad, another fellow musician, though the older girl had a different bio-logical dad, the two girls were raised as if they were biological sisters. Elyssia was the older daughter, a brunette who had a kind spirit and the younger of the two, Selina, who looked up to her older sister and referred to her with a cute lisp as "Sithy." Elyssia would see her biological father once in a while but knew him only as part of an extended group of musician friends acting more like an uncle or older friend to the group than her dad. Elyssia had never felt bad about the situation because she was treated like an equal with family and friends who never al-luded to the idea that they were anything other than

100% sisters. When Elyssia turned about ten, Jasmin started seeing changes in her daughter. Elyssia began hearing voices and becoming paranoid, one time even falling down the stairs because she thought a witch was chasing her. Her mom struggled to find someone to help with the situation but was hitting a lot of dead end roads. She eventually got her prescribed Neuthatrotin that seemed to work for a while. Soon after this Elyssia was visiting her dad with her sister, by now Jasmin and he had split, and he had a new woman in his life. For the first time in Elyssia's life, this woman began referring to Elyssia as a "Stepchild" reminding Elyssia that she actually had a different dad and for the first time in Elyssia's life, she began to feel that she was different and not really a part of the family unit. It got so bad that this woman did not want Elyssia coming to their house anymore and Jasmin remembers her daughter and her watching Selena drive away to the other house while Elyssia sat peering out the window in despair as Selena and her dad slowly disappeared into the distance. The memory was hard for Jasmin to describe because I could tell the sting still stung to this day. This prompted Elyssia to begin rebelling and the combination of teenage rebellion and mental health issues were a recipe for disaster that led into a lifelong whirlwind of hospital visits, counselors, and manic episodes.

Early on she was diagnosed with bi-polarism but that soon changed and she was diagnosed as schizophrenic. She would have moments of clarity but then there would be the moments of delusional thinking that led to actions like her turning on the stove one night and then abruptly taking off feeling as if she was being watched leaving the potential for a fire. She had a friend down the street that had access to her dad's liquor so they started drinking, which in turn, led to her hanging out in the wrong crowds and more than often older guys. Her behavior was getting worse over time and more irrational. At some point, Jasmin's family had her picked up from Juvenile Hall and had her taken to a facility in Utah. A consultant had arranged the transportation and education for a small fee to the family of 300,000 dollars. If that sounds like a lot of money that's because it is and that is Jasmin's complaint about the entire industry of "Treatment." She confided in me that there is a total lack of programs to treat a dual diagnosis. If you enter a program and need to be treated with Psych meds then these centers do not want to treat you for drug and alcohol issues simultaneously. She was supposed to receive a psychiatrist to get an appropriate diagnosis but that never happened they instead tried to punish the kids in the facility pushing them to hike and used disciplinary treatment that only resulted in her running away from the treatment center with her parents short 300,000 dollars and Elyssia with a total mistrust of the medical system.

Jasmin made a point to express her total disappointment in the mental health system and claims that they missed the window of opportunity to help Elyssia. She explained that if your child was having an episode you could not take them to the emergency room unless they are expressing suicide tendancies at the time of arrival or alternativly, they would put them on a three day involuntary lockdown that is so tramatic for a person and scares them into not wanting to seek out future help which, most of the time, doesn't consist of a follow up anyway. She suggested these are more crisis centers as opposed to health centers. She believes that there should be education and behavior interventionists that help with explosive behaviors before situations decline to a lockdown type of scenario. Her main gripe though is that she emphasized that these facilities need to facilitate dual diagnosis programs. Most of them will not treat addiction of alcohol and or drugs along with any psychosis issues which she found to be the number one hindrance of her daughter getting treated successfully because while she did need antipsychotic drugs, she also needed to treat the effects of addiction. Like most people dealing with these types of mental problems, with extreme highs and lows, reality flashing into delusions, these people often rely on other drugs like stimulants to keep them high on any of their low days. And she said that these facilities, at least at the time, were not able to hone in on more than one diagnosis therefore there was a failure in the entire system.

But these episodes began to get more intense and Elyssia began disappearing for days then weeks at a time only to reappear with a phone call explaining that she had hopped a train and was in a different state now. She had a little network of friends, fellow musicians, addicts, people who had run away from home, and they spent their time train hopping riding the rails to wherever the wind blew them. A dangerous life but a very exhilarating one as well especially for someone who craved that adrenaline rush.

At some point, Elyssia became pregnant and had a son she named Tyler. During this short period of time she seemed to have stabilized a bit and had gotten an apartment and was caring for him. She was fulfilling her motherly duties while staying off the streets or in facilities. All was going well until one night when Tyler was six months old and she left him for the first time intrusted in the care of her biological dad and his wife who was a nurse and tragically he unexpectedly died from SIDS or some unspecified heart condition. Elyssia was devastated and slowly returned to her unstable ways of disappearing, one of her specialties, and the nightmare only intensified when her boyfriend she had been dating went to look for her in New Orleans where she had fled to but tragically died along the way of a drug overdose. Now there were two dead where there had been only one and that combo sent her into a tailspin with no end in sight. More episodes, delusions, drugs and alcohol until Jasmin got a call one day that Elyssia was in the hospital with liver failure. Jasmin jumped on a plane and was told that she could be a donor for her daughter if her daughter could manage to stay sober for a full year. During this time period I saw Elyssia outside of the grocery store in San Francisco bumbing change and she looked very unhealthy. The rebellious girl that had always reminded me so much of myself was just a mere resemblance of her old self, her looks and demeanor had been plagued by alcohol and drugs and mental health problems. Having been around addicts my entire life, and having had had alcohol issues myself, I knew nothing I said was gonna help because you just have to get sick and tired of being sick and tired and, though I have a penchant for trying to save everyone, I knew at this moment my efforts would be futile.

Jasmin never gave up hope and sent word back to the Mayan priests she had left in the Yucatan where she had been living prior to the call and those prayers must have sailed across the seas for Elyssia ended up surpassing that time clock and lived another three years without ever even being able to get any long time sobriety. Jasmin was with her daughter holding her hand to the very end and watched her slip away to the other side where I'm sure there exists a kindler and gentler world.

Jasmin teaches again and looks for solitude in helping others. She reiterated that they need to democratize health care by treating it in three tiers for a successful outcome. She explained Tier one should be the mental health education with Tier 2 helping someone when signs first appear with any treatment that might help such as therapy, meds, or anything else to treat the diagnoses before it spins outta control and lastly the third tier that is the crisis services when all other attempts have failed by dealing with the patient in a kind and effective way based on individual needs. She's still happy and has good days along with the bad. The sad part is that they had finally found a facility that accepted and treated dual diagnosis in Berkeley, CA and in the month leading up to her death her name was finally selected from the waiting queue but unfortunately her time had run out waiting on the waiting list but I know her spirit is still riding those trains into the night while the wind whips through her hair and street poetry whispers prose from the night sky.

Gay Parents and the Taboos That Have Accompanied Them....

The world is changing and most people are accepting of the fact that same sex couples are people living under the same stars as everyone else and they have the same dreams and desires as straight couples. Typically they have had to overcome adversity in their own lives navigating their way through ever changing social norms that evolve everyday. I believe that the internet has been a positive outlet for gay people in general allowing their voices to be heard all across the world even in places where they would otherwise be hushed. But love is love and people fall in love with people for different reasons and sometimes the reason has no explanation.

Times have been changing for gay communities in a mostly positive way. Today gay marriages are legally performed for same sex couples in 36 countries around the world with most recently Napal and Estonia joining the list. There is still room for improvement because 35 countries still don't allow this under their constitution. Some even still consider homosexuality illegal and it is criminalized.

China and Russia are two countries who forbade even the advocacy for same sex marriage claiming that it threatens their national culture. But these places are strict on many more issues other than gay marriage while most other countries have been moving more and more towards tollerance of different sexual values. The first same sex couple was married in 1971 in Minnesota and slowly more states began legalizing same sex marriages.

Most countries that allow same sex marriage also allow for adoption between the same sex couples. The research done shows that financial, psychological, and physical well-being of gay people are benefited by a marriage and that the children of these couples benefit from the union as well taking away the stigmatization and discrimination. But gay couples are no different than everyone else and sometimes things fall apart and their unions come to an end just like any straight couples dissolution of marriage. When divorce is the only answer they will need to have their issues solved in court about custody rights and other issues that couples going through a divorce face.

For now gay parents have become more socially accepted and I don't believe we will ever turn back and not have same sex couples adopting kids or using surrogates and whatever other means they use to achieve their dreams of having a kid. Kids just want to be loved and in the end they just want to be in an environment that is loving and healthy no matter where or who that love is coming from. Gay parents can provide stability and guidance to a child and be their guiding light leading them into their future.

Adoption...The Long and Winding Road....

Every year thousands of kids are adopted through the adoption process. Sometimes this evolves out of fostering to eventually adopting the foster child and other times patience is required navigating your way through domestic and international adoptions. It is estimated that one in thirty-five kids are adopted annually with 50,000 adopted within the foster system alone. Out of all the children adopted, 49% are male while 51% are female which seems like a pretty balanced statistic. Sometimes circumstances can tip the scale in one direction or another. After China made it a law that you could only have one child, many girls were put up for adoption because parents favored males that could carry on the bloodline making international adoption of these girls commonplace here in America. Overall statistics suggest that of all kids adopted here in the states, 37% are white, 23% black, 15% hispanic, 15% asian, and 10% other. So there is a wide range of nationalities that are being adopted as well as a range in the adoptees themselves. Many times cultures cross in the process resulting in multicultural families.

In Gabrielle Glaser's book American Baby, she claims that for many women adoption has been more of an obligation instead of a choice if you were a poor single woman that had found herself unexpectedly pregnant and unwed. Chances are that you would have been hidden away in a maternity home or made to live with strangers working as a servant until the baby was born and then the baby would be adopted out into a closed adoption. This type of adoption would not have included a post-adoption agreement that allows for communication between the child, the adoptive parents or biological parents, moreover, it was a done deal. Once someone came to lay claim to one of these unfortunate non-privileged female's babies whose mothers had made the mistake of getting pregnant in less than favorable circumstances, they would take the newborn and that would be the last time the mother would see her child. Now, 60% of births have some type of post-adoption agreement attached to the adoption. Gabrielle also went on to say that after World War II, three million babies were funneled into the system by parents not really fully understanding the process itself and that some were simply just desperate suffering from the casualties of war.

Times have changed though because people began to believe that kids would fare better staying closer to their cultures and peoples and they began to be raised in their homeland more frequently instead of automatically being brought to America just because there were wealthier people here willing to pay a lot of money to get a child. Just the other day, the Supreme court voted in favor of upholding the 1978 law called the Indian Child Welfare Act (ICWA) by a 7 to 2 decision rejecting a challenge by a white Texas couple who argued the law was a form of racial discrimination when they were attempting to foster a 5 year old girl after already adopting her older half-brother. The Navajo Nation fired back claiming that the law helps protect their traditions and cultures. The ICWA was put in place 45 years ago to address a widely spread practice in the 19th Century by the US government and states of taking children from their Native American families in order to assimilate them into white America. Obviously Native Americans have been unfairly treated since the beginning of our history so it seems like a good outcome for past injustices that have left a stain on our national history.

Adoption overall is a positive option for couples that can not conceive themselves but are desperate to have a child that they can call their own. And it goes both ways because it offers an avenue for a pregnant mom to have a different path besides abortion where they can assume that their child will be well cared for by a loving family providing him or her the best opportunities for a successful life. 62% of children who are matched and placed in homes are newborns and under one. Statistics show that the reasons for adopting vary with 81% simply wanting to provide a permanent and stable home for a child, 69% wanting to expand their family, 52% not able to have one biologically, and 24% wanting a sibling for one of their kids. And the background of these future parents vary as well with the average age of the adoptee being 44 and most having some sort of college experience, a BA or higher, while only 9% having less than a high school diploma. This makes sense because children are extremely expensive to raise and a college education would generally enable better paying jobs that could help cover the costs of school clothes, food, college, entertainment, and a lifetime of doctor and dentist visits. The average cost to raise a kid from birth to 17 is about $275,000 which is no pretty penny. Though this statistic is financially staggering, combined with the fact that a child can be emotionally taxing, a surprising 93% of domestic adoptees said that they would do it all over again. It can't be overstated enough that kids can be a big pain in the a** sometimes, however, most people believe that the rewards of parenthood outweigh any, if not all, of the negative aspects that accompany it. In the end, it's not who birthed you that's necessarily important, more-so, who raised you, that will leave a lasting effect on a kid's life and society in general.

John Castrana- A man's perspective and adoption journey.

____

So as to protect the anonymity of the child I have changed the names of the dad and daughter in this interview. I wanted to interview a male to get their perspective on the adoption process that can be long and tedious as well as taxing on a relationship. So for this interview I have named the dad John and his adoptive daughter Gia. And so the story goes… . John and his wife were living in Manhattan and wanted a child desperately but for reasons I am not privy to, they were unable to become pregnant. So for about six years they entertained the idea of adoption keeping all avenues open. Finally they decided this would be the road they would take and spent the next year or two getting all their ducks in a row to make it happen. 60,000 dollars later, their dream would come true and they would cross state lines to pick up their beautiful daughter Gia. The process was anything but smooth and was full of wrinkles from the get-go but the greatest rewards in life unfortunately sometimes must derive from the biggest challenges and obstacles.

First of all, like I have already mentioned, there are many paths one can take to adopt but John and his wife opted for hiring an attorney to help with the process. Not only an attorney but an agent as well that helped talk them through the entire process. His wife and he were instructed it was mandatory to make a booklet that would describe through pictures and illustrations just who they were as a couple by including personal touches to help the birth mother envision what her child's future life would be like with the new family she chose. The pressure was on because this book was their lifeline to adopt a child. They knew they needed to present themselves as a responsible couple who were interesting, stable, and kind. Each photo would be chosen meticulously to portray them in the best light possible because they would be competing with plenty of other parents anxious to adopt a kid and everyone knows first impressions are key in life.

So after constructing their favorable book, John told me he was informed that it would be a good idea to set up a phone line that was designated solely on connecting with a birth mother. Each state has different laws on adoption, some more strict, while others more lenient. An example is that some states allow the birth parents to reconnect with the child after ten years as well as many other differing details and laws so they were determined to choose a state that pretty much sealed the deal in stone once they got the baby so there wouldn't be any chance they could lose the child to laws that were designated to favor the birth mother. Sounds harsh but these situations are very touchy and adoptive parents struggle alongside the birth mother in the adoption process leaving both having to do a lot of leg work to make the transaction successful.

Next the ads are run in publications such as church newsletters and city agency pamphlets containing pregnant moms looking to put their child up for adoption to be matched up with couples who were looking for a baby. So the ads are printed then sent out and the parents wait patiently praying for a pregnant mom to choose them based on their booklet's beautiful presentation of what they will be like as parents.

When John and his wife were chosen by a birth mom their excitement went through the roof. They were so excited they could hardly contain themselves. The process was rolling along now at a nice speed and during this time someone was assigned to come to their house to interview them asking questions like what religion they were, what type of food the baby would eat and check to see if the house was clean etc. It needed to be established by social workers that they were deemed safe and reliable enough to care for a new baby. There was tons of paperwork to be filled out and loose ends to be tied together that became a very time consuming endeavor that can leave parents feeling emotionally drained. All this time and effort ended up being fruitless though, for when they finally went to the hospital when the mother went into delivery, the parents of the girl having the baby threatened to disown her if she gave her baby up for adoption. At the last minute they were denied the child that they had so patiently waited for and the blow was hard and devastating. John's wife cried uncontrollably because she had planned on going home with her new baby and now they would be going home empty handed.

This is how the process goes though. There are no guarantees and you must remain patient and calm or you can have all your hopes dashed. So there they were at the starting point once again with their polished booklet waiting to be chosen again. They were on the line financially because they were responsible for paying attorney fees for themselves and the potential birth mother, hospital bills on top of airline fees and advertising. Basically just a lot of different receipts that add up as the process goes along. This is not the road a lower income person or family could take. It hits the pocketbook hard and pulls on the pursestrings like a nagging kid wanting candy. But they persevered and when another birth mom showed interest they were quick to establish a relationship with her and the union grew stronger over the next few months until it was decided that they would be the new parents of her baby. John and his wife crossed state lines but once again and holed up in a hotel for a month or so in advance of the arrival of the baby to ensure this time there would be less chance of her changing her mind at the last second. John also shared that a counselor sits down with the adoptees and counsels them on strategies to deal with a new child and that they encourage you that if you should get a child, you should keep most of the details about the birth mom private. They don't believe it's anyone's business why the child was given up for adoption and all the circumstances that surrounded that decision. They also go over what ages the parents might want to address the adoption itself to the child and that if a child was of a different racial background it should be addressed even sooner so that the child will not be confused by the differences. Being that his daughter would be of a mixed race, they suggested K-first grade would be a good time to address it otherwise it would have been between about 7 or 8. John added that later when he did tell his daughter Gia about having been adopted, she did not seem that fazed by it but every six months or so she would have a new question until slowly over time the questions fazed out all together.

The day finally came after long days waiting in a hotel room where his daughter was finally born. His wife and he in all the crazy pandemonium realized on the way to the hospital that they had forgotten to get a baby seat for the car so on the way to the hospital they had to detour to a local Walmart and get a child seat to take the baby home from the hospital in. He remembered upon entering the hospital they were overcome with emotion and excitement. John said the second he entered the room and laid eyes on his daughter Gia he was delirious with joy and the moment their eyes locked he felt that this was his daughter. There was no going back and since that day he has felt a great love for her and the insurmountable love compares equally with the love he feels for his biological son he eventually had with his new wife after he split from his previous wife that he had adopted Gia with. He made it clear that he felt an instant love for Gia and adoption did not lessen any feelings of parenthood as she had been his all along.

There were rules in place that they could not take the baby for about two days, he couldn't remember exactly but the state wanted to make sure that the mother was not under the influence of birthing drugs and was in her right mind when she signed the adoption papers. But then that was it, the papers were signed and they were driving away from the hospital with Gia, happy new parents of a new baby girl. He recalls having to go back to the state after about six months for a checkup of the baby ensuring her well being was being attended to and that her birthweight was ideal and she was clean etc.

Overall he admitted this was no walk in the park. There aren't even any guarantees you will be chosen by a birth mom. He shared that they could never celebrate the moments leading up to the arrival like other parents because they were always worried the rug would be pulled out from under them like it had been the first time. The adoptions can be opened or closed which will dictate the rights of the birth mom after the adoption goes through. All said and done John expressed no remorse in going about it the way they did though it enevidably was expensive and stressful because the outcome gave them their beautiful daughter Gia, and though the marriage with the adoptive mom didn't work out, John has remarried and had a biological child with his new wife and claims that Gia loves her brother and there doesn't appear to be any jealousy within the big new blended family. His final words on the matter were that if someone was considering adoption they should just go for it by any means possible and that if someone was worried that their feelings for their adopted child might pale in comparison to those of a biological child born through their bloodline, they will be pleasantly surprised because the bond feels just as tight if not stronger because you have been blessed with the special task of caring for this beautiful being. Today Gia is a beautiful striving teenager with a whole future in front of her and John is a happy dad dealing with the same issues all parents of teenagers deal with, adopted or not, and his love is all-consuming and never wavering.

Big Families. A Curse or A Blessing...

My Grandparents and my grandmother with some of her brothers and sister

Big families have mostly become a thing of the past. Where once you would see houses filled with a bunch of kids, now three of them seem like a big family. Most parents don't start having kids in their teens or early twenties so there isn't even time now to have great big families because a lot of people are waiting til thirty or plus to even start a family. Especially in cities where you are limited to living in flats and apartments there is just not room for dozens of pitter-pattering feet to be running around. I know there are famous people you see like the Duggars who were on a popular show 19 Kids and Counting that are in the public eye who have a big family, and possibly more out in rural areas or in very religious families that do not believe in birth control, but for the most part, especially here in the US, I would say this is more of a rarity than the norm. And even though these families seem happy on TV, we have learned over time that they are plagued with problems as well. The Duggars have had to face many scandals that have made their lives seem anything but perfect but when I was growing up I would have given anything to be part of the Brady Bunch's family that seemed to be a big happy family when their show came on every week. Living in San Francisco I do experience a lot of three-generational families living in the same home while at work especially within the Asian and Latino communities. Many times grandparents live in the homes with their kids and they bring their grandkids out to my school bus doting on them waving as I drive off. But there still aren't ten kids running around the house sleeping four to a room sharing beds.

Big families of the past would share in all of the work to help the family prosper. If you lived on a farm everyone would be expected to pitch in on fieldwork or duties within the house. Some would be instructed to tend to the animals milking the cows and collecting the eggs. One meal would be made and that's what you would eat like it or not. Hand me down clothes were absolute and if you were a younger kid you would have never experienced new clothes.

I grew up spending summers with my grandparents that were the best memories of my life. My grandfather was an immigrant that came over from Italy with about ten cents in his pocket. Back then only some members of the family would come over because there was not enough money for everyone to ride the ship that would carry them here and the ones that came first would establish themselves and then send for the others when the time was right. My grandfather came with his dad and they did not have a pot to piss in. They spoke Italian and did not have a lot of skills needed to get good paying jobs but when they finally settled in they sent for his sister and mother. The immigrant story then of landing at Ellis Island and then trying to assimilate into society was a tough and hard transition that was not for the faint of heart. My grandfather fought the odds and ended up eventually going to pharmaceutical school and becoming successful because he worked tirelessly trying to make something of himself and learned the language and prospered. By the time I had arrived, his family was all gone. His dad had died by suicide, his mom was dead and his sister had been put away in an assylum, though at those times, it was all very hush-hush and no one talked about it. He was a mild mannered man who sat back on the couch quietly smoking his pipe and taking everything in with his eyes rather than needing to fill the silence with words and noise. He seemed to keep his feelings to himself and there was no talk of his family members.

My grandmother in comparison, was a whole different story. She had come from a gigantic family and had fled with all of them during the war from Germany. She had so many brothers and sisters it was hard to keep track of them all when they would come by everyday on those warm summer afternoons on my summer break. They were all very touchy feely and I always ended up being pulled onto one of their laps gasping for air because my uncles would be drenched in cologne. My aunt Babe would grab me and squeeze my cheeks and plant a big wet kiss on my face leaving behind a big red lip mark. She had been the type whose face was a little overdone with makeup and I always saw those huge red lips coming from a mile away. There was Uncle Carl, Aunt Pat, Aunt Babe, Uncle Ben, Uncle Henry, Uncle Alex, Aunt Kaia, and others that I didn't even meet. When they would be together they would be talking so loud as if they were at a party where everyone is drunk and talking over each other. They all spoke to each other in German, a language that sounds very aggressive, almost obnoxious, from a child's ear's point of view. My grandmother would be on the phone with them all day if they weren't at her house and you would be able to hear her from three rooms away talking and laughing for hours at a time. There was a real comradery between them and they were all very involved in each other's lives. I don't remember a lot of fighting but I'm sure there must have been because that happens within all families. They all went on trips together and all of it was put on reel to reel film and every summer the first thing we would do is get the projector out of the closet and watch all the home movies of all of them visiting Canada and other places that they had traveled to always smiling away and hamming it up for the camera. The contrast between my grandfather and grandmother was stark and there was definitely a different attitude between the two of them. It seems that because my grandmother had been from such a big family, and been exposed to them all the time, that it really played a big part in shaping her vibrant personality, whereas my grandfather had been more reserved and sullen.

My grandmother and grandfather had worked tirelessly their entire life like most immigrants do. They had to come here and learn the language and build something outta nothing. My grandfather had opened a pharmacy in a drugstore and my grandmother ran the soda fountain in front just like you see in the movies. They worked day and night only to sleep a few hours and do it all over again the next day. They penny- pinched shopping at cheap stores and my grandmother always clipped coupons when I was there even after they had become successful. Many immigrants had stood in bread lines in their home countries, seen war up close, and often had one outfit to their names so they were frugal, always prepared for the rug to be pulled out from under them leaving them hungry and cold again. There was never any waste and she had cabinets full of old whip-cream containers and coffee cans filled with home-made cookies. People back then were not wasteful especially if you had come here with nothing but the clothes on your back. Your work ethics were all you knew and you were fully aware that when you woke up in the morning your day was gonna be long and tiring.

My days spent there during my summer break were the best. Spending time with her big extended family made me feel whole. There was never a lonely moment because someone was always arriving as soon as another was leaving. We made homemade pasta that we dried out all over the house for my Italian grandpa. We ate tons of German food with potatoes and sauerkraut and my grandmother would make her famous strudel treat. These are my first-hand memories of the experience of being around a big family that I will always remember fondly. It was a much different vibe than most houses I'm at now that have much smaller families because most people can't afford to have tons of kids or just don't want the responsibility of taking care of them. But back then, it was more common especially if you were from an immigrant's family and I will always feel blessed to have gotten to experience that.

Autism.....The Challenging Road Ahead...

Autism affects so many families, and now more than ever, the numbers have increased to questionable levels. Why have the numbers increased so much? Is it because in the past it wasn't recognized by parents or professionals? Did we miss the signs when they were right before our faces and pass them off as "Oh your child will catch up, they are fine?" And in missing the signs did we miss early opportunities to intervene and begin intervention because early intervention is supposed to be an effective way to guide a child to success. Or is the problem something entirely different? A lot of parents believe Autism is caused by the immunization cycle that kids must endure as young as newborns but that ramp up in their early years. Rounds of Hep B, Pollio, Influenza, PCV13, chickenpox, and Hep A vaccinations are just a few that are injected into your young blood stream seemingly all at once. Some believe that the myriad of different medicines is a recipe for a disaster on their kids' immune system and that their fragile systems cannot handle all of these at once, if at all. So you have the anti-vaxxers out there that have taken their grievances to facebook and other sites complaining that their child should not have to take the toxic cocktail for them to go to school. Is this a justified argument? There was a measles outbreak in NJ in 2019 among the unvaccinated that left some claiming that it was irresponsible not to be vaccinated. So it is definitely a hot topic that has parents on both sides of the argument very emotional and passionate because many swear the vaccines caused their kids autism. And if it's not caused by genetics or vaccinations, some just believe that environmental factors are causing the rise in numbers like dirty polluted air and water. Many studies have been held and many doctors and scientists swear that tests show that vaccinations are not causing it but personally I don't know if I'm buying it because I've known a lot of friends or acquaintances that claim that they noticed a change in their kid immediately after getting the round of shots and their life would dramatically change. And so here's a story from a mom who's been there, a first hand account. Her child rides on my special ed bus and is so sweet. His favorite thing to do is take selfies of himself before he gets on my bus, and he has to take them before he gets off. On his way out he grabs my arm and caresses it and says "I'll be good I'll be good." It's neither weird nor creepy, it is just part of his routine and who am I to get in the way of his routine?

Kids with autism do not like their routine disrupted. I drive kids on all different levels of the spectrum of autism. Some you can barely tell they have it while others have traits making it obvious such as repetitive hand movements, covering their ears, and making repetitive words or sounds but these are the telltale signs that I recognize by their short bus ride. There are other signs as well such as no eye contact, no big smiles, very little back and forth gestures such as pointing, reaching or waving, little or no response to their name, few words or meaningful phrases, preference for solitude, not wanting to receive hugs, and lining up toys and other items in a methodical ocd way. When you see the signs on a day to day basis you begin to recognize them quicker and tune into each child's different way of interacting with the world seeing it through their unusual lenses instead of your own.

So then, it is of dire importance that we begin to recognize the signs as early as possible to help kids adapt to their own personal worlds providing them with the greatest potential for success in their lives while simultaneously digging deeper into the mystery of autism so that at some point we can cure it and kids and parents won't have to live with their child's sometimes crippling and challenging disabilities.

Enilda and Ricardo.. A mother's love...

Like clockwork, I rolled up to Enilda's house in the morning. She was always timely bringing her son Ricardo out to my bus and he was always in a good mood taking one, two and three selfies of himself as she followed behind him while he entered my bus. She watched him sit down and made sure to remind him to seatbelt himself in because he was distracted with the selfies. As we heard the seatbelt eventually click, Ricardo and I and the other students were rolling off again off to their High School. When we eventually made it to the school I would let the kids disembark once I saw the teachers waiting for their students at the open gate. Ricardo was always the last one off because he had to get his last selfies in and then as he would get off my bus he would reach for my arm and give me a couple repetitive rubs and say something like "I'm a good boy, I'm a good boy" while bobbing his head up and down and then proceeded to exit my bus for the day and I would close the bus door and make my way to my next stop. The kids on this pull were some of my favorites of the year. One child and I had a special connection and would conversate everyday about what was going on in his life from his moms car getting towed, his teeth being sore and his family's plight trying to find avenues to have him treated by an affordable dentist to trivial things like how his twitter account had been shut down and his disappointment that he lost his followers for gaming. I feel so blessed that I get to work with kids everyday because, though our time together is short, I get to share in their innocence that is so refreshing. I go out of my way to make our time together special. I know that their days start with me and end with me and if i can be a positive light in their day I'm gonna shine bright on them because maybe other parts of their day will be stressful, hard, and not so bright.

For Ricardo's mom, she does not have the same luxury of other parents where they see their kids off to school and then they come home at night and entertain themselves by playing sports, video games, doing their homework, and watching Tv. Instead, as soon as Ricardo drives away on my bus she must quickly use the few minutes she finally has to herself and gets ready to go to her job at the city-college. As soon as she gets off, her work will continue until she goes to sleep. Ricardo needs constant care and attention when she gets home. He needs her help with most tasks and needs to be supervised even in the shower which she admits has become awkward now that Richardo has grown into manhood but a moms love knows no bounds and she knows it's just something she must do. He has a rare skin condition known as hidradenitis superlippahua that leads to sores under his arms and private areas and she is tasked to put ointment on these areas daily. She helps him clean himself in the shower, helps scrub him down in the bath and most likely, though I didn't ask, needs to assist him in going to the bathroom. When I interviewed her Ricardo was still in the background needing to be supervised to make sure he was safe and entertained and she treaded lightly because he understands if she is talking about him.

She is separated from his father and he was their only kid. I asked if she had wanted to have another kid but she said that she decided that it would not be fair to Ricardo because the doctor warned her that the chances of her having another child with autism was as high as 50/50 maybe even higher and she believed that these odds would have him not receiving the proper attention if he had to compete with another brother or sister that would require her utmost attention so that dream was dashed and she decided that he would be her only child.

I also asked how the dad and extended family dealt with the blow that yes, Ricardo did indeed have autism when it was finally determined. It had taken a while for someone to finally diagnose him.

She told me that it had been a totally normal pregnancy having had no signs of problems except that he was born a little prematurally by three weeks. He walked at eight or nine months and seemed to be progressing normally and everything seemed fine. At eight months he had his MMR round of shots and developed a very high fever. Before this he had loved to babble and after he recovered from the horrible fever she noticed a change in him. He stopped babbling and his personality and demeanor drastically changed and he became silent. By two he was still not progressing, engaging or playing normally with toys and at this time his preschool teacher suggested that he be evaluated because she had noticed his corky way of lining up toys and his knack for repetition. She told his mother to always go with her gut feeling when it came to her questioning if something could be wrong with her son and that is one of the main takeaways I got from her. She said that parents must go with their gut feeling because there will be many teachers, doctors, and other personnel that will pass it off as "Oh your child is fine '' when you might know deep down in your heart that he or she isn't. These children are often not affectionate, wanting hugs or kisses and often find true solitude in being alone.

Ricardo never cried. First they thought maybe his hearing was off because he also wasn't talking.

So at 3 ½ or 4 they had a speach and hearing specialist check to see if his hearing was ok and finding it was normal, that was eventually ruled out. More dead ends. Her primary care doctor promised her that her son was fine saying "NO, no, no he's a boy that's how they are, he will catch up to the milestones and be fine." But she was not buying it because a mother just knows and the gloom and doom set in for she knew something wasn't right. Finally a specialist wanted to do a round of developmental tests and finally she was delivered the news that she had been dreading all along that Ricardo was indeed autistic and his mom said that she would place him somewhere in the middle of the autism spectrum that varies from barely on the spectrum to barely functional. She told me that in the past only about two in 99 children were diagnosed with it while presently the statistics are 53 in 99. So yea a huge difference?

So back to the extended family and his dads reaction because she told me that once she was given the diagnosis that she herself was almost relieved by finally being vindicated on what she had known for the past couple of years and now she was determined to do whatever she could to help him on his more complicated journey. She said the dad was somewhat ok but of course he was a sports guy and now his son would never be a star quarterback or leading pitcher but that he was accepting of the facts and tried to deal with the prognosis the best he could. Unfortunately, the older Ricardo got, the more resentful he became with autistic traits that screamed at him through Ricardo's actions combined with the lack of normalcy. When his son was 16, he left the family home. His family had a difficult time with it as well although everyone tried to play the part of a supportive family member. Enilda's brother and sister live with her now and lend their support when asked but she feels that this task to care for her son is primarily hers and she tries not to burden them with the never ending job of caring for him. He has had a few violent episodes where they had to step in because, with Ricardo reaching manhood, he began to physically challenge his mom and it's gotten so bad she has been left with bruises from the altercations because she says that she is no match for him now because of his strength. She believes that Ricardo has kind of reached some plateau and realized the pain he inflicted and it has deescalated the problem somewhat where the outcome is less brutal. His dad still calls once in a while but the conversations are limited to hellos and goodbyes without much content in between.

It's heartbreaking to know that one of his biggest achievements in life is being able to assist his mom at making microwaveable popcorn though it's something positive and sometimes in life you have to be grateful for small achievements. At school he was learning new tasks to prepare him for an adult world like helping at a local grocery store stacking cans and food items. But unfortunately Ricardo will never be able to take a bus by himself like some kids on a different scale of the spectrum are able to do after graduating out of the school system. Ricardo is 21 so now he is phasing out of the SFSD school system that only supplies help for these special needs kids til they are 22. From there the parents need to get them into access programs that will continue to meet their needs like a place that I drop older kids off called the Pomeroy Center in San Francisco. There they help older youth and young adults adapt to the work world to help facilitate the individual enabling them to participate in more programs but it can be expensive and parents initially need to be referred by the Golden Gate Regional Center and many times you lose your case worker and there is endless paperwork that's exhausting and tedious on top of an already daunting task of caring for your grown adult child. If you pay outta pocket it can be as expensive as 1500 a week so it is imperative for parents to jump through the hoops to make sure that they receive some kind of governmental help.

So what does the future hold for her small family? As I picked up her kid recently for his last trip on my bus, as he snapped his last selfies, and administered his last arm rub on my arm, his moms eyes looked tired knowing that she might have to quit her job now that summer had approached since she does not have a placement lined up for someone to care for him while she is at work. She says that her days are all consuming as soon as she gets off work because as soon as she gets home, she is on again taking care of her son until she might get a half an hour to herself once he finally goes to sleep. Her entire life will probably look like this which has made dating near impossible when they see the amount of attention that needs to be paid to her child that will likely leave little leftover for them.

Hopefully we as a country will spend a lot more on resources for this desperate community of parents dealing with children with autism. Hopefully we will find a cause and make sure no other family has to suffer from this abnormality. There are definitely angels living among us and I believe Enilda is living and breathing proof of that and I can only hope her circumstances find her with all the help she could ever need. It was a pleasure meeting Ricardo and being able to provide him with a little sunshine everyday in an otherwise gloomier existence.

Single Moms and Dads...
Is One The Loneliest Number?....

Single moms and dads are just as prevalent now as married couples. Marriage can be a tough pill to swallow for many and making it last requires compromise and mutual respect of both parties. There is absolutely no room for selfishness. It can be a very positive aspect of one's life and some people fall in love and spend their whole lives married to the love of their life celebrating all the anniversaries along the way. Some believe you actually live longer when your in a marriage as opposed to living alone but marriage requires teamwork and understanding and men don't usually see things the same way as women so when we think that they should just, "know how we are feeling and act accordingly," the fact is that they usually have no clue that we are even upset until we explode leaving our feelings spewing all over the place like hot lava rolling down the side of a volcano. "Nobody said it was easy," and that might be the understatement of the year. Even if you were living with your bestie every day of every year dealing with kids, bills, heartache, insecuries, addictions, depression and the list goes

Cheryl Norman Cordero

on and on because those are the things that people have to deal with on a daily basis. And then you have to cohabitate with someone while dealing with all these emotional issues and usually someone starts to project all of their baggage onto the other person to relieve some of the tension they feel. It's like offloading cargo and putting it on someone else's ship to deal with. There are so many struggles a couple faces whether they are straight, gay, bisexual, whatever, they will face uphill battles in marriage. Sometimes things are great but then sometimes they are dreadful. Some people have supportive partners who are always there to lend a helping hand while others are cold and often shut down. Some people are clean freaks while the others are total slobs and this can become a big problem. Some people are night people and some wake up at the crack of dawn and, though this doesn't seem like a big deal, it can be. If one is always ready to go out at night they will become resentful if the other one never wants to go out and be social.

People in relationships can develop addictions to gambling, drugs, alcohol, porn, sex, and all sorts of other things that will lead to cracks in the relationship. Not only are these people generally sick from their addictions, their partners become sick along with them and often become enablers. Addictions can have the addict spending all the money that is supposed to be delegated to rent, mortgage, food, or things for the child and many times the addict can lead the family into bankruptcy. It's a very slippery road and no one in the relationship will come out unscathed.

Sometimes parents become single because their partner dies or is killed and many times this happens suddenly leaving a grieving parent that not only has to keep on keeping on for themselves, but they have to ensure their child can move through the grief and get past their loss. Once in awhile a parent will commit suicide and and, when they do, it is hard for family members bear. The survivor can become angry at their parent for leaving them behind and some blame the dead person for ruining their family. Sometimes they are filled with an intense grief that they can't shake and go over and over the event in their head many times blaming themselves or others for the outcome.

So many people nowadays are plagued with mental problems and are medicated and many end up blowing off those meds leading to some unstable behavior. They can become violent towards their partner and very erratic. This puts a lot of pressure on the other person and can be very scary for them because some are just not equipped to deal with huge swings of emotions. A lot of people have affairs in marriages and at times want to leave the relationship to be with the other person. Sometimes it is a mutual breakup but many times one person wants out while the other is devastated and can't believe things are coming to an end. They spend years obsessed with the other person trolling their social media sites and trying to find out everything they can about the other person. Sometimes the kids get dragged in the middle and suffer the consequences.

Today is just a hard time to stay in long term marriages. Life is very hard for a lot of people and sometimes their husband or wife takes the grunt of it. It is so hard to keep love alive in a world filled with so much hate and anger, jealousy and unrest. But hopefully when things do fall apart, people will find the courage to pick up the broken pieces and move on with dignity and grace. That's always easier said than done but everyone has a lot more strength than they give themselves credit for. The best case scenario is that a couple is able to work through their issues, ride out the ups and downs, and walk happily ever into the sunset.

Dave P. and his son Jay...
A single father journey

The Golden Gate Bridge stretches 1.7 miles over the San Francisco Bay with Alcatraz as its backdrop that was once the home of the worst criminals in the United States. Trolley cars have been a staple of the city for many years as they climb and descend up and down the rolling hills while passengers snap shots of all the sites. You have Twin Peaks that displays a view of the whole city, Golden Gate Park that is a sprawling paradise, and the city is home to many famous districts like Chinatown, The Castro, the Mission, and of course, Haight Ashbury. Chinatown is home to thousands of Chinese immigrants who came here for a better life landing at Angel island waiting for their applications to be processed. The district boasts tons of dimsum restaurants, Taoist and Buddist temples, and once a predominant gang organization that was referred to as the Tongs. It was basically a city within a city with the Chinese people occupying the area controlling their own legal affairs, banking, and handling of new arrivals. The area also had a seedy vibe to it with gambling rooms, erotic massage parlors and opium dens tucked away in little crevices throughout its neighborhood. Today it sees millions of tourists every year looking to visit a good noodle house and purchase a Chinese souvenir like a shiny new kimono. Once a year there is the famous Chinese New year parade where you can catch a glimpse of a man-made walking dragon as well as dozens of illuminated floats and lanterns and witness an array of music and dancers celebrating Chinese history.

The Castro is planted in the Eureka Valley and is associated with gay culture. Many gay bars are open to customers and many who frequent them are the LGBT community that have found the bright and colorful neighborhood dawned with big rainbow flags a safe-haven for their culture to flourish. Any given day walking the streets of the Castro you might see men in drag, men and women in leather chaps, naked people sipping coffee, same sex couples, and many other interesting people that you probably would be less likely to see walking down the street in places like the midwest but here, people are open-minded and are not phased by the diversity. The Castro Street Theater is a landmark that often has a multicultural and LGBT focus on its entertainment. The Castro is also home to many boutique style restaurants, alternative bookstores and adult shops making it a fun place to visit if you're not a resident. Every year in October is the Castro Street Fair that was founded by Harvey Milk and is a day celebrating Gay Pride with lots of music, dancing, and speakers of the LGBT community bringing the city together no matter one's sexual orientation to engage in the diverse culture.

The Mission was a place of rebellion during the 60's with proponents of Cesar Chavez being voices for change. Fruit stands, taquerias and bookstores line the streets and street art muralists have made their mark on their neighborhood. After 1979 Families would prepare all year for the yearly Carnaval celebration that celebrates their culture with festive music, lowriders, and dance. This section of town is blessed with a lot of sun and every weekend residents flock to Dolores Park to bask in the heat, picnic in the grass, smoke weed, hula-hoop or engage in some recreational activity. Many weekends you'll see lowriders cruisin the strip while their cars hop, three-wheel and hydraulics lower them to the ground while the oldies blast from their car speakers and bands like Santana, who's lead guitarist spawned outta the Mission, play as the cars cruise on by.

Haight Ashbury is as famous as the picture of the Beatles walking across the crosswalk on one of their famous album covers. It is known for its eclectic group of people roaming its street where hippies, hipsters, and homeless people and their dogs grace the street with their soulful presence. Tons of second hand clothes stores adorn the street like Held-over and Wasteland that have been around for many years. You have a Ben and Jerry's Ice Cream shop that gives a nod to the Grateful Dead Band that roamed the same street years earlier with the ice cream named Cherry Garcia. When I first moved to the city over thirty years ago the street was buzzing with musical excitement with partygoers and musicians hopping back and forth from Murio's bar, The Nightbreak, and The Ibeam when bands like Short Dogs Grow and House of Wheels were filling the club. At the end of the block was a bowling Alley that we used to go play a drunken game of, "see if you can keep the bowl in your lane," but now has been replaced with the very popular Amoeba Music that is a must go to for vinyl heads and anybody who is a true collector of music. So if you are looking for an Instagram photo selfie of yourself in front of a

Haight Street sign waving a peace sign or you want to go buy a pipe in a headshop, this is the neighborhood you will want to visit on your next trip to the Bay Area.

The sixties in San Francisco was an onslaught of musical genius while hippies wore tye-die, smoked weed, dressed in bell bottoms and flowers in their hair, many rebelling against the Vietnam War. This was the place that people flocked to from around the country looking for free-love and mind altering drugs like LSD. Musicians like Jimmy Hendrix, Jefferson Airplane and Janis Joplin would all play shows in the panhandle, a strip off of Golden Gate Park and then continue to party all night with the other wayward kids in some flat in the Haight district.

The Black Panther Party was developing right across the Bay Bridge in Oakland Ca that was an African American revolutionary party formed in the wake of Malcom X's assisination in 1965. And finally we come to Dave's story after my nostalgic walk through San Francisco's history.

It was at this time that Dave was growing up in this city that was pulsating with manic energy. He had been raised here all his life and at the ripe old age of 17 he met a nice girl from a neighboring Catholic girls school and they began dating. He had been attending Galileo High that OJ Simpson had begun his football career at. A year later she found herself pregnant and it was at this time they decided to get married because that's just what you did at the time. She had been from a Catholic family of Spanish and Italian heritage living in North Beach right by the famous Catholic Cathedral across from Washington Square. You could guess that her parents were anything but pleased with the pregnancy news but Dave did his duty and married her at a small ceremony at the courthouse that was followed by a small intimate dinner reception for family. She had not even graduated from high school yet so when Dave went and got an apartment, she stayed back with her parents to finish out her senior year before moving in with him.

Both families were old fashioned and expected them to raise the child together as a married couple. After she moved in with him the baby was born and they named him Jay. Dave said he had been happy being a dad and had helped his new wife with the parenting duties helping her feed him and change his diapers. Before this he had been living a more wild life at one point working as a gas station attendant right by the famous Avalon Ballroom that showcased many of the famous bands of the time. A lot of the touring bands would park their tour buses or vans at the gas station that Dave worked at and let him come down to the shows via the backstage entrance. He watched a lot of the greats play and one night he caught a glimpse of Janis Joplin walking in the alley towards the club with what appeared to be a flask of whiskey in her hand and as she breezed by Dave he held out an open chip bag for her to get a handful of chips but as she passed by him she grabbed the whole bag instead with a brazen smirk. But he had had a lot of wild times up to this point but now his life was becoming focussed on taking care of his wife and new son.

She got a job as an operator because at that time 1000's of operators were needed to handle all the calls going through the system that is now a thing of the past. The switchboards would light up all day with collect calls, emergency breakthroughs and making connections with callers. Dave worked nights on movie sets while she worked days as an ekg tech so they would often cross paths passing off the baby to one another. Three years in when Dave was 21 or 22 the tensions began building and they decided to separate after three years of bouncing around in different apartments trying to take care of Jay while working.

In 1975 in the height of the disco era, when cocaine replaced LSD and mushrooms, San Francisco had a whole new vibe going for it and the whole hippy thing had died overnight. Dave decided at some point that instead of renting he would buy a house for himself. When he made the purchase he chose a home situated blocks from the beach and houses away from Golden Gate Park and it was then that his wife decided that that option sounded a lot better than staying behind in the apartment by herself thus deciding to move to the house with him. Even with all the promise of the new house things fell apart one year later when Dave came home his son told him that a man that she worked with at the hospital had been hanging out over their house. His wife had been an EKG tech and was also attending nursing school and her new boyfriend Bob was an X-ray tech at that same hospital. She really wanted to experience her youth and wanted to party and do what other people her age were doing so Bob became the new man in her life. Dave told her that if she wanted to be with him it wasn't gonna go down under his roof and told her she would have to go live with Bob. At that time Jay was given the option to go live with her and Bob or stay at the house with his dad where he had been living and Jay quickly chose his dad and stayed put.

Dave settled into the life of a single dad. He said that dating was a little tricky and that a lot of women were not interested in taking on the role of a new mom. It was the 70's and women were more inclined to go to the discos, doing a line of coke, and dancing the night away to the Bee-gees or Saturday Night Fever soundtrack. But Dave carried on and dated more casually and lived the life of making sure his son had food and a roof over his head. Dori, their neighbor, was a mom to many kids and if Dave would work late she would always have a door open for his son. Dave's mom also lived conveniently nearby and was always happy to help out with her grandson. Back in those days most kids were latchkey kids whether or not there were two parents in the home. Jay learned to be self-sufficient making his meals and getting himself around the city. He would go visit his mom like twice a year for about a week with the prodding from Dave because Jay and his mom had had a bit of a continuous relationship because she had really taken partying and drinking too far at times. She eventually died at 68 and it seems that she did not carry a huge burden of regret for having not played a bigger part in her son's life.

Dave still lives in the same house on the same block he's lived in since 1975. When Jay was graduating high school Dave told him he could go to college and he would help pay for it or he could get a job and contribute around the house and that's what he did. Dave said it wasn't a super affectionate relationship with hugging all the time and I love you's after every phone conversation but that they rarely fought and Jay knew that he was always there for him. Jay eventually bought his grandmother's house out from the other relatives and moved in a few blocks away from his childhood home. He has a wife and they had a son so the cycle continues. Dave gets to see his grandson all the time and feels they have a close bond. His son still comes by several times a week and hangs out with his dad at his house. I asked Dave what was the main message he would convey to a new single dad ready to embark on raising a child by himself and he said patience, communication and honesty are the key elements of a successful relationship. He added that really knowing your child is important and making sure your relationship is built on trust. When Jay comes over Dave instinctively knows when Jay is not wanting to talk about something any further and he will drop the unwanted subject without even being told to because he just instinctively knows to. It was Jay and his dad all throughout his adolescence and now they still walk side by side in his adulthood but they are now blessed with one more generation with his grandson being the new shining light guiding them into their journey into the future.

Younger Moms Vs. Older Moms, Who's To Say?....

Some girls get pregnant in high school and some women wait til they have their careers before they get pregnant. Sometimes these pregnancies are planned while other times not so much. So what is the perfect age to get pregnant? When kids have kids some people look at them and wonder why the hell they would want to ruin their life by having to take care of their kid instead of chasing their dreams. It's not always easy trying to go to class when you have a baby to nurse and watch after and trying to get homework done is probably difficult when there's a screaming baby in the background demanding your attention. And then when you graduate and have to get a job, you're horrified that daycare is so expensive because you usually start off making minimum wage. It makes it hard to make ends meet. I have known a lot of young moms growing up and most seemed to like having a kid and many stayed with their moms until they could afford to move out on their own. Almost all the young moms I knew did not end up staying with the fathers of their kids if they were ever together at all. Most raised their kids by themselves until they eventually met someone else and then they got married and some had more kids with their new partners. Pregnant and 16 and Teen Moms somewhat popularized and normalized the whole idea of being a young mother and was a hit show on TV. It gave teenagers a birds eye view of what it is like to have to care for a baby at such a young age and probably scared off some while others were probably intrigued because these girls on the show kind of became stars and they probably got lost in that watching the show. I will say from experience that these young kids have the energy to do it whereas as you get older you begin to lose some of that youthful energy that keeps you charged all day.

Older moms have become more of a trend. I think a lot of women want to be independent and don't want to be tied down to a screaming baby. Many women want to go to college and then they want to start their careers from there. A lot of women are waiting to get married until a little later in life and then they wait a couple more years til they have their kids planning every step along the way as if they have cliff notes for their life; college til 24, career till 30, then get married at 30, and two kids 34 and 35. Check. Check, check, and check. Everything is very structured. A lot of women want things to be perfect. They have their toddlers in a bunch of playgroups, they have two breast machines on each breast to get milk for their babies, and they are making homemade baby food and jarring it for their little ones.

So who's to say what age women should reproduce. It's a personal decision and women generally have the option nowadays to choose what is best for them. Accidents do happen sometimes and women get pregnant unexpectedly, but even then, some get abortions because they feel they are not ready to be moms and for whatever reason they don't want to go the adoption route. In the end, everyone should choose at what age they want to bring a child into this world and not let anyone judge that decision.

Small towns are notorious for everyone knowing everyone else's business but they usually keep the gossip within their own small community. You often hear whispering voices quietly saying, "Did you hear about so," or "I think Mr. Allbott was over at Mary's house," at the grocery store or at the local tavern. Everyone seems to have something to say about everyone else, but when push comes to shove, most of the town is very loyal to one another and when strange faces show up in town, everyone takes notice and looks at them with skeptical eyes and mouths become more tight lipped. Hadley grew up in a town like this. She told me her personal story and was willing to give me a peek into life within her small town experience.

She is eighteen years old and grew up in Eureka, Missouri. Her life started off ill-fated because her dad had died a few months before she was born in an untimely death at 21 when he had been killed in a bad car accident. Her mom was devastated and gave birth to Hadley while she was still living with her mother. She explained to me that she comes from a long line of young mothers and that both her great grandmothers were still alive. I asked her if this was typical in her small town and she told me that she knows of three or four other girls living there that are eighteen and getting ready to get married who plan to have kids right after the wedding. She went on to say that her mom ended up meeting another man and they got married and had a kid, a baby brother. Apparently her mom developed a drug problem and became addicted to pain killers and other drugs and her life really began to spin outta control. One day her step-father came home from work and found her mom in another state of mind under the influence of pills and he freaked out leading to a huge fight. Her brothers and her were in her bedroom huddled together when her mom came in weilding a gun and said "Don't worry, I'll handle this" while they stared back crying, scared to move. Hadley tried to shield her baby brother from the out of control scene, hugging him and protecting his young eyes from his mother's rage. By this time her mom turned her sights on her target and chased the dad out the front door taking aim and shooting. Lucky for him, her aim was off and she missed hitting him while his back was turned scurrying off. The cops were called and she was arrested. Her mom had only been seventeen when she became pregnant and obviously she was a young mother making bad choices. Hadley said that her mother had seemed to seek out men that could help provide for the family and that while this man helped fill those shoes, he had also been abusive towards her mother though he was not an addict himself. One of her mother's ex's dads was the local sheriff so he was able to get the incident somewhat 'swept under the rug' but Hadley was sent to live with her grandparents for close to a year until she was able to return with her mom. As time went on, old wounds healed and her mom reunited with her step-dad and once again they were all living together. The town folks probably had some gossip to talk about but went about their business like small town folks do.

She was your typical teenager and started smoking pot with her older brother at thirteen. At that time weed was frowned upon but she was curious and began drinking alcohol as well, sneaking out of the house to go out and party with other kids. She had sex for the first time when she was fourteen and confessed that she didn't use protection and didn't feel necessarily guilty afterward though it wasn't something she had pursued. She stayed in a relationship with the boy she had become intimate with for two years. During this time period she had moved to a bigger city with her family, St. Louis, Missouri because her step dad had gotten a better job in a factory. She had been commuting back and forth between St. Louis and her hometown so that she could see her boyfriend but he eventually broke things off leaving her broken-hearted.

Hadley told me that she had never been good in school and suffered from bad asthma that kept her from recreational sports or hobbies that would have been affected by her condition. Living in St. Louis, she ran away from home one day when her step-brother and dad got into a fight and she felt old feelings creep back up reminiscent of the turmoil from her childhood. She ended up calling CPS and letting them know about her step-dads behavior so she was not able to go back to her family's house and ended up staying with another family becoming interested in the church and the life of a missionary even though both of her parents were atheists. She had a new boyfriend and things were going along smoothly for the young couple when she became pregnant. They both decided, though she was now religious, that they did not want the baby and she had an abortion. She said that she still feels guilty about it and sometimes her boyfriend and her cry about having gone through with it. I personally know other girls growing up that experienced the same guilt and regret about getting an abortion that were still regretful after many years while I know others who don't regret it at all and have moved on with their lives. But weirdly enough, she got pregnant again only months later and this time they decided that they were gonna keep their baby and so that brings up to her current state of being six months pregnant. Her boyfriend works and makes good money as a car salesman and they live with his parents who apparently don't know she's pregnant because it is a dysfunctional family that has turned a blind eye. She says she doesn't try to hide it but no one has said anything to her about it and they are in the process of looking for a new apartment to move into to get ready for the arrival of their new child that they yet to know the sex of. When I asked her if she was happy with her decision to keep it she said that she felt that it was meant to be but she was quick to add that she really didn't want more biological kids because it was too hard with pregnancy and continued feelings of being isolated and lonely. She told me that she was open to adoption in the future and was planning on enrolling into college to become a social worker and that she was prepared to juggle the responsibilities of being a girlfriend, baby, and student though she knew it would be challenging. She is secure in her relationship and doesn't feel any need to rush into marriage even though some of her relatives that still remain in her hometown are asking when the marriage is gonna happen. She always reminds them that some of them are divorce and she will get married when the time is right but for now she is satisfied with the way things are and she is patiently awaiting for the day of her baby's arrival. Her mother is now apparently addicted to adderall and went from being about 300 pounds to currently about 90 pounds. Addiction is a problem in America whether you live in a small town or a big urban city. She does not hold judgements or resentments towards her and only hopes she begins to love herself and get sober. And like John Mellancamp's song lyrics, "All my friends are so small town, my parents live in the same small town, My job is so small town, provides little opportunity," seems to say it all and why she's living in the bigger town that has her boyfriend making a good salary and what ultimately keeps them from moving back to that small town but she still embraces it's charm and travels their frequently to see her family and friends and someday might live there again with her new little family.

Cheryl Norman-Cordero...
But who better than me..

My Husband, myself, and our Daughter

Well, but who better than me to tell her story about giving birth at the young old age of 45 years old. But for most women that seems like getting in the game a little late but I had already had two boys when I was younger and I was never one to shy away from a challenge. Never one to take it too personally when people would look at me weird after I told them my age when they would ask while I was pregnant. Their stares went from my protruding belly up to my face then back down again to my belly then over to the younger dad then managing a fake smile that looked more like a bewildered shriveled up prune, but you know, I enjoyed watching people skirm. I grew up with junkies and losers, not to be judgy, because I was doing the same thing in my high school. We were the ones that went to school only to meet up with the other losers, pick up the drugs, and in my case avoid my perverted dean, and scoot off to some party at a kids house by the school whose parents were at work or hitch a ride down to the river to a place that we named "The Log" to drink all day and ride on this board that was tied to a tree that was like a surfboard on the flowing water. If we had one too many we would venture over to the little island, usually swimming back later in the day under the influence and possibly blacked out, so yea, not a safe combination. So I was pretty used to being a little different than your average Joe or Sue or whatever.

When I found out I was pregnant I did not want to keep it because I figured that it would piss everyone off but my boyfriend wanted me to so I decided that I would get on board and take the wild ride. Apparently there is not a huge group of women coming into the hospital pregnant at 45 so the doctors were concerned about my health. They wanted to perform extra tests to determine if the chromosome counts were right and that the baby's health was intact. One nurse came in and told me that most women that came in at this age ended up miscarrying their babies and that I should not get my hopes up because the odds were not in my favor. I was thinking to myself, "Ok let's see, I went on tour to Europe 4 or 5 months pregnant and played punk shows every night with drunk people and girls with their nipples pierced and mohawks and skinhead dudes chugging beer cans all night then driving around in a tour van from show to show in a foreign country. Yea, I think I'm good." When I got back into the country I remember landing and the guy checking my guitar bag for contraband looked at me and my big belly hanging out of my cutoff half top like "What the hell is wrong with you?"

But in all seriousness, I feel like the pregnancy was a smooth process and the birth was the same as the other two had been, me having to have a c-section because the doctor's said that since I had already had two, it would be the safest bet. It wasn't all rosy because mainly I did not want to have to stay in the hospital as long as I did because one day is all I can stand in a dark windowless room. But when they performed the c-section and my girl was shown to me, I felt happy because she was my first and only girl and I hoped we would have a great relationship. When I was younger I assumed that I would struggle with a girl because I was more of a tomboy type but as I grew older I knew that I would be a good mom to a girl. We had her name picked out already. She would be River Marie Norman-Cordero. River because I had always loved River Phoenix's name and Marie was her father's mother's middle name so it was decided and agreed upon and set to print on her birth certificate.

I found the first two years very hard. It was only hard because honestly I'm not a baby person. I'm not mesmerized by the cooing, I don't like changing diapers, getting up all night, and quite honestly breastfeeding is not for me even though I'm into totally natural things. I was also never a fan of the playground where groups of moms would sit around all day snacking on celery sticks and their kids carrot sticks and talk for hours about what color their kids poop was or what their little boy's sleeping schedule was. But hey, "To each his or her own, it's just not for me." But once River turned like 3 or 4 I became enamored with her. When she could put her own clothes on and communicate without a tantrum I was right there by her side ready to ride or die. Boys and girls are completely different to raise. I don't know how to explain it but they are just very different personality-wise and consequently I found her to be very easy to be around.

Out of all of my three kids, I believe River has been the easiest and not because her dad has been in the house helping me raise her but because I am older and this has made it easier for me. When I had my first kid I was 28, had just been on tour and did not want to be settled down yet. Even with my second 8 years later I don't think I was ready for him either but I know that River would be my last so that made her special plus I had no desire to be out partying every night. I still was traveling and pushing her around different cities while my then boyfriend, now husband and kids skateboarded but it wasn't like it was when I was planted on a barstool every night. I was much less selfish now and I wanted her to grow up with some stability. However, don't get me wrong, each kid of mine has a special place in my heart. I have my oldest Lane who I've always referred to as "First born," who was the one who dealt with the majority of the drama of his dad and I. When he was young we were in between houses because we had went to LA to live so I could play music and once I got there I was miserable and we went right back to SF. When we came back we had no place to live and nobody wanted to rent to us with a pitbull so we had to sleep on some girls' floor in the basement and then when we had to leave there we spent time sleeping in our Forerunner in Golden Gate Park. One night we were sleeping and someone managed to break the window and steal our stuff while we were sleeping which is surprising because I'm a really light sleeper. Another night I had been watching a documentary in the back of the truck on a little tv that was charging on the cigarette lighter about how we supposedly never really landed on the moon. It seemed convincing enough at the time, lying in the back of that truck trying to fall asleep, until I finally did. I was awoken by cops knocking on the window and a light shining through the window. I squinted my eyes and when I finally got it rolled down, I offered my new knowledge and let them know that we never really landed on the moon and they just looked at me like I was crazy and told me that I couldn't sleep in the park all night so I got into the driver's seat while Lane slept and drove on to the next spot. But times weren't all bad. He got to go to our shows when our band played and sell merch and hang out with a lotta cool people. He was on soccer teams, got to go on trips and lived in pretty nice places along the way. Of all my kids he was the smartest and would score in the top 10% of the US on all of his tests in school. He was and is a great skateboarder and always challenged himself to skate better. His brother Chase, who everyone called Bubblz, was a different type of kid. He was much more mellow and had a funny sense of humor. He does not remember all that much of his dad being around, he grew up more with my husband and they skateboarded all over the town together. Whenever Cody and I would fight he would be the go between and always would have something funny to say. He was my wing-man from day one. He always had my back. Sometimes he would enter skateboarding contests and I loved to watch him skate. You know how some people get into some kind of competition and choke, well he was quite the opposite. He would start skating and skate better than I had ever seen him skate flying in and outta bowls and down staircases with absolutely no fear. River also has a great sense of humor and has brought great joy to everyone in the family.

So wrapping up my interview with myself about having a child when I was older, my daughter has been a very rewarding part of my life. I feel blessed that I somewhat proved the doctors wrong and she was a healthy little girl. I am 54 now and she's eight so maybe I will look a little older than the other moms at her graduation but knowing me, I will most likely still be sporting a short dress. She made me laugh the other day when she came home from school and said, "Mom guess what I learned today, you are the oldest mom in my class and dad is the youngest dad," and I was like "cool" I like pushing the norms. I will continue to try and gain knowledge to raise my vibration. I'm a senior at San Francisco State University now trying to get my degree in Anthropology because that's what interests me. I would love to get a job in the field of Anthropology or a job helping to find missing kids. Whatever I do, I will give it my all and keep putting new goals in front of myself. I believe the meaning of our existence is all about love and that we are all one.

Family photo with my kids and husband

Band Pics: Squat and at Slim's with THe Nightcrawlers

*My old band Squat Promo shot and
on the streets of New York*

Squat, The Lowdowns, and The Nightcrawlers

Surrogates... Who Will Do?.....

Surrogacy in the US is one of the most assured and convenient means to find a surrogate mother in the world but it is also one of the most expensive as a result. This is where you can find the most advanced IVF clinics around with the most resources for couples. If the baby is born here in the United States he or she will immediately be issued a birth certificate and will have American citizenship.

The US is known for its advanced medicine and groundbreaking technological advances. If a baby is born here in the US it's chances for survival are far greater than in other less modern countries. About 80 percent of embryo transfers result in pregnancy when donor's eggs are used which is great statistics compared to other overseas clinics. Clinics are required by law to report their success rates that can really aid in a parent's decision on which clinic to choose when deciding to find a surrogate and begin the process. Most programs range anywhere from 140,000 to 160,000 which is a hefty sum for most families and state laws vary about who can find a surrogate. Some allow single people while others only allow for married couples. Some explicity allow only hertrosexual couples though that will probably change in time.

A Surrogacy agreement will be drawn up that will cover financial arrangements and terms of the surrogacy itself. There is also a Pre-Birth order sometimes that instructs hospitals in the third trimester to draw up birth certificates with the future parent's name so that there is no chance of a surrogate's name being inscribed instead.

The process is all scientific and there should be no room for error. The mother's egg is used and is fertilized in a test tube by the father's sperm and then the egg is placed in the surrogate's uterus. She then carries the baby to term and then hands the baby over to the parents once it is born. No DNA from the surrogate is shared so the baby's genes will be from the mother and father only. Though this can be somewhat impersonal for a couple or single person, the outcome usually outweighs these emotions and parents are usually overjoyed that they are now new parents when most of them were unable to do it without the help of a surrogate. Most of the time the surrogate has been financially rewarded and has known and come to terms with the arrangement for months so they are generally ok with handing over the baby to the awaiting parents. This process is a long process as well as expensive, but if one has the means to do it, it usually will produce the child that they've been dreaming about. Once in a while there is disappointment when IVF does not take and there is no fertilized egg to implant but in plenty of instances it does make people want to give it a shot and hope for the best. We are coming up with new technological advances everyday so hopefully the future holds even more advances in the field of conception and more parents that are having problems conceiving will have even more options moving forward.

Baby Steps Into Our Future.....

With over 8 billion people spread out across our planet, some doomsdayers believe that there are too many people here on Earth and that it is causing irreversible damage to our fragile ecosystem. We have plastic accumulating in our oceans at unprecedented numbers killing off our marine life, global warming is causing extreme weather leaving the skies a burnt-orange hue from massive wildfires, and sea-ice sheets are melting away causing rising waters threatening low-lying cities that will soon be overtaken by the sea on the shores they are settled upon. Everywhere we look there seems to be some sort of collateral damage caused by human behavior and many believe that we are overpopulating our planet and that it would be in our best interest to stop having so many kids.

"Is overpopulation wreaking havoc on our big blue planet?" We read the articles, as crazy as they may sound, about farting cows that are being over-produced for human consumption, that are producing toxic air but that's nothing compared to the air-pollution caused from factories that are leading the pollution problem. Fossil fuels from cars are also damaging the biosphere making us rethink our energy usage and pushing us towards electric-vehicles and motivating us to shut down pipelines that are bad for the environment. Since the Industrial Revolution our population exploded and has been expanding, that is until very recently. In 2000 the world's fertility rate was 2.7 births per woman, above the replacement rate of 2.1 that is necessary to keep a population stable but today it is 2.3 and falling.

"Oh shit, what the hell does this mean for us?" Maybe the reality is that we are actually on the decline with birth rates dropping rapidly leaving us with a more prevalent older population while there are fewer young people having kids. "How will this affect us going into the future?" Experts on the subject explain that that could be a problem for the older generations because pensions draw from a younger workforce paying into the system to cover the seniors' checks. The youth are also considered the risk takers and it is believed they are the ones that come up with the forward thinking ideas needed for new discoveries in health and science. They are the explorers and without them we might become somewhat stagnant in the fields of technology that advance our society as a whole.

People claim they want more kids but when push comes to shove couples are finding the skyrocketing cost of living is making it impossible to have a lot of kids, if any at all, and some women just don't want to have a flock of kids to take care of. Housing shortages don't help entice couples to want to start families and some women still struggle with fertility problems and the ones that are giving birth find they can't afford daycare when it is time for them to return to work. The wealthier a country gets, the less kids it produces. Wealth leads to fewer people having kids and thus, we have older populations. Poorer countries tend to have more kids but many are uneducated living in rural areas that don't provide the standards of education that lead generations into the future. While immigration has helped ease the worker shortage in the US and other financially successful countries, these workers are coming here and are typically only able to fill jobs in areas such as agriculture, childcare, and the food industry but bring few doctors, scientists, or mathematicians.

This is not to say that these people do not bring value to a country but they are not gonna be able to assimilate, at least for a while, into jobs that produce a major economy. It has been hypothesized by psychologists that younger people have "fluid intelligence" which is the ability to think creatively that enables them to solve problems in entirely new ways. I guess that older people aren't thinking about creating as much as settling in for retirement and we need as many young minds as possible to keep us fresh and thriving as a species. So a shortage in "fresh blood" might keep us stagnant as a society.

"But who's to say?" The Black Death kept our population numbers in check while the Coronavirus rolled through countries taking lives with it. In 1918 the Spanish Flu claimed over 50 million lives changing the way people think about their connection to their own mortality. When the Coronavirus hit I don't believe communities were able to accept that we could still be so affected by a virus in this day and age with most people feeling invincible from them and flu like symptoms that we blindly assumed science could eradicate quickly, however, we were quick to find out that we aren't immortal and are only human. Its effects are still felt currently. I feel like the impact of sheltering in place for so long with people having been trapped in their homes, some people all by themselves, made us feel vulnerable, lonely, and at a loss for control over our own lives. I believe these feelings have lingered past that stage and we now all think a little differently knowing that the reality of some apocalyptic type scenario is more possible than we once might have thought and who knows when the next pandemic will hit and what societal changes it could bring to the human race.

I guess the key to keeping population growth lower without the biggest impact on civilizations is education. Africa's reproduction pool is ever growing but we need to make sure that it is being educated and uplifted. Two-thirds of Chinese children live in the countryside with inadequate means for a good education so schools need to be implemented even in more rural desolate areas. Very few of India's millennials have finished secondary school and until we, as a collective people across the globe make learning the number one priority, we will continue to fall short and the implications will include later retirements, lower real-estate returns, higher taxes, and government budget crisis along with the already mentioned potential shortfalls.

To continue the discussion I must add that AI could totally change the playing field. We might actually need less people moving forward because AI could take the place of many people that would have otherwise been needed to be tasked to a certain job that a future machine or robot will eventually do. It's sad but true we will be replaceable but there will still be the need for new generations to rise from the ashes of older ones to replace the people that have come before us. Unless AI learns to reproduce itself, that will more than likely happen, we'll see more specialized machines and humanoids learning from themselves to adapt and make improvements along the way and we'll need the gene pool to keep doubling or tripling to keep up with the demand in all areas of life. Or…. could it be that we would be better off if we were catastrophically hit by an asteroid or something killing off a lot of people giving the human race a chance to start anew and the earth a chance to recuperate. So we shall sit back and listen if the future wields babies cries or the biotic squeaking from body parts of an AI creature. Until then, one never really knows.

Thank You, But No Thank You....
and The Big Heartbreak

Some women don't end up having any kids at all. Some just simply don't want them. They feel content in their lives without having to bear children and chase them around a house like some Tom and Jerry episode. It's as simple as their biology does not outweigh their desire. Many women are career driven and don't want to have to slow down to the speed it takes to balance motherhood with a job or school. Some grow up watching other moms and their own moms struggling to keep it all together wearing all the many hats a mom has to wear. Some women feel resentful that the stereotype of a woman includes her bearing children. Other women are quite the opposite and they are desperate to have kids but as fate would have it they have been un-successful at getting pregnant. They wait to look at their pregnancy test every month waiting for it to turn the right color and, when it finally settles into the "Not Pregnant" result, they break down in tears on their bathroom floor feeling defeated and angry. Some go through in-vitro fertilization treatments and sometimes it just doesn't take. They go through hell and back, always hoping and praying that this will be the time until it doesn't. Other women simply just never find the right person or the right time. Whatever the reason, it has been seen as a kind of taboo in the past and some women would have been discarded and replaced if they couldn't have a kid to carry on the father's name. Times have changed though and women are more in charge of their own lives to do as they please and the future will probably offer even more choices.

Pamela Aujulo . . .
55 years young and childless but ok

So as I wrote earlier, I was in an all girl punk band that was one of the first all girl bands that came outta the whole Riot Girl genre. There were other bands that came before us like Bikini Kill and The Lunachicks and some that we played shows with L7 and 7 Year Bitch. When I was younger I spent my days with skateboarders, drinking and watching bands play but I wanted to be playing myself and not on the sidelines being a spectator. So I met a girl named Pamela, if I remember right, at the Haight Street Fair, and she became the lead singer for our band. We had started out with a different vocalist but she was not in sync with our attitudes of,

"I am woman hear me roar," or our style, we wore boxers shorts, cut off jeans, wife-beaters (that term probably is off the table now) and most of the time went makeup-free. This was almost thirty years ago and this was pushing the norm at the time and that's exactly what we wanted to do. We were consciously trying to make a statement that we were tough, didn't need some guys telling us what to do and that we could play as good as them. My views have softened now and I don't feel resentments towards men especially because I have two boys and I've seen how in the last couple years men have really been picked apart and I just believe it comes down to acceptance that we are the ying and they are the yang, or vice versa and our biology sets us apart from one another and it's of no fault of our own.

The first time the original singer came down this staircase at our first show, I believe it was at a Berkely campus party, she was donned in all these frilly clothes wearing thick makeup all over her face like some scary scene out of a movie like Mommy Dearest's Joan Crawford's character descending from a spiral staircase with a long cigarette holder in her hand hopped up on speed and we were like, "Uum what the hell happened to you" and "Yea, that's not really our vibe" so we went with the girl I had met at the fair instead. Let's face it, we weren't playing some pretty music we were playing punk and like Mike Ness said, "That's back when punk rock was dangerous, before you could walk into a mall and get your little pussy pierced, or your little Doc Martens boots, or your crazy hair color." She was some tough looking sexy guitar player that ended up being one of my favorite female vocalists of all time. She cruised around on a motorcycle and didn't take shit from anyone. She was a Peruvian goddess with long thick raven curly hair and tattoos so we knew we had our girl. And later she reminded me that she also had a van and that made her all that more enticing because we needed to be able to get our equipment around and put up show fliers around the city before the internet made doing all that legwork unnecessary.

We got a set together, started playing shows, and we were electric. I think we just had "That Thing," that you either have or you don't and lucky for us it was the former. We kept getting bigger and better shows by meeting more and more people in the music scene. Our friends were all musicians and that was just our life, practicing and writing songs everyday till all hours of the night in this music lockout called Lennon Studios. Our rehearsal space was envied by other musicians because it was the coolest of the lot. It was a loft and to get to you would have to climb up a ladder and then crawl through a hole in the ceiling where you would find yourself in a huge space with big skylights as light poured down on you as if you were a star in the making. We had band posters of all the local bands and shows plastered to the walls and after every show we would have a bunch of guys come back to the loft with us to help unload all the equipment back up to our space using ropes while we watched the guys who were now our groupies hoisting Marshall stacks and all the drum pieces up one by one through the little trap door and then one by one all the after hour parties would come marching out of the hole like little ants coming outta the ground. Generally the last arrival would be the big ice chest full of beer that we would then circle around to help manuever through the opening as it were precious breakable cargo. We would continue to party into the night after our shows until someone passed out or ended up puking. We toured the US and Europe and it was during this European tour that I left 5 months pregnant. Of the only two shows I decided not to play, one was one night in Austria when the show had been moved and our driver was instructed to follow some guy on a bike that said he knew where the new venue was as we preceded to follow him over rivers and through valleys on his bike while our driver drove behind him in our van. We laughed hysterically listening to loud classical music while this old man rode along gleefully smiling, seemingly unmoved by his tiresome task leaving us baffled and feeling like we would never get there but this poor man continued peddling away while waving us on. At some point we arrived at a huge castle and our tour van made its way down a path underneath it. We walked into this room and there were all these low doors that a troll couldn't even fit through and plastic sheets hanging from the ceilings like a horror movie. A bunch of strange people were walking around dragging their legs and we were like, "Ok, there's some weird inbreeding going on around here," and it being so cold, I decided not to play the show that night.

On another night we arrived at a gig and realized that some of our equipment had been left behind at the hotel that we were staying at so we decided to go back and get it. It wasn't that simple though, because we were in Europe and the steering wheel is on the opposite side of the car, and our driver had stayed back at the club leaving our bass player to try and navigate her way back to the hotel. Whenever I wasn't playing I tried to save my energy and I was laying down in the back of the van while the bass player was driving and the drummer was navigating using a prehistoric paper map. Yes, this was before GPS made it easy to get around in foreign locales. They began arguing about the directions when the argument came to a head and the drummer ripped up the map. The clutch was making grinding sounds while our bass player drove recklessly and aimlessly through a town we had never been before. I finally sat up like an awakened corpse and tried to be the peacemaker but the map was in pieces and we were forced to find our way blindly through winding streets and past signs that were in a different language and impossible to read. We did manage to retrieve the missing equipment, and by some miracle, we made it back to the club before we were supposed to play.

I kept on playing shows every night and tried to sleep part of the day. At least it kept me sober through the tour but one night some punk kid peed in a cup and set it on stage as if it had been placed there by club staff. During the show I reached down and took a sip and spit it out when I realized what it was. After the show my band and I were worried that I could get sick from drinking it but I never did. I had only continued getting bigger and bigger every day until we returned home from the tour returning looking like a Weeble Wobble.

Pamala was an amazing songwriter and guitar player. Although I was always saying I didn't want kids, I somehow ended up with three. So at 55, I asked Pamela to tell me about why she never had any kids when we had been on the same life course for so long but at some point we took two different paths at the fork in the road.

In her words she explained to me that from a very young age she did not want to have kids or get married. She had no visions of walking down the aisle in a flowing white dress while guests stared on in awe. And like me, oddly enough, she remembers getting a gift that had an impact on her, similar to the one that had spooked me. She was gifted a big box set that had some plastic high heel shoes, a broom, a mop, and an apron. She was mortified. She had watched her Peruvian mother work tirelessly around her house and she had no desire to end up like that and have to give so much of herself working as a stereotypical "Housewife." She was a free-spirit and had bigger plans for her future than to sit around dusting and cleaning for some possible ungrateful husband and bratty kids. She wanted the "House" without the word "Wife" attached to it.

I asked her if she had any regrets now about not having kids and she did not hesitate to reveal that she didn't have any regrets whatsoever. I then asked if she ever felt sad on holidays like Christmas or Mother's Day and she told me that she just doesn't feel like she missed out on anything. She shared that she had nephews to spoil and that satisfied her maternal instinct playing out the mother role with the option to drop them back off when she wanted and that was good enough for her. She went on to explain that she would never have been able to do the things that she has done had she had kids to take care of adding that she had picked up and went on tour at 46 and had always relished in the freedom to be able to pick up and go anywhere on a whim. Ever since I met her, she's always been fiercely independent. She admitted that she never wanted to have a child for the wrong reasons such as outta boredom or because of low aspirations. She was fully aware of the commitment it would take to raise a kid between the expenses and the emotional support that would be needed to provide for a child and the daunting task of being responsible for someone else's well-being and happiness at all times. Knowing her like I do, I know that whatever she takes on in life, she wants to do it well.

She did volunteer that there had been one time in her adult life where she had been in love with a guy, that type of love that has you giddy wanting to be with that person every second of everyday and began entertaining the idea of marriage and a kid but the relationship had ultimately fell apart before any ring or baby bundle.

But still, no regrets. She now lives with a man that has older kids and seems content with her life. She's traveled extensively, worked different jobs, remains independent, and is getting ready to be-

come a stewardess and suggested I might do as
well, but my eight year daughter demands more of
my time than I would have traveling city to city on
a plane so there u have it. She has the freedom still
to do as she pleases and her story continues as she
readies herself to take to the skies on a new adventure on this seemingly endless journey of life.

Karie Marriott...Sometimes the stars don't align as we would like them to....

When I spoke to Karie about her being unable to have a child I could tell she was gonna be emotional when we got into the details. She is a very kind person who has spent much of her life doing things for other people, helping out friends and family, and working hard so this is why she asked herself at times, "God, why haven't I been able to have a kid when I've done all the right things and been a good person?" But we all know this isn't the way the world works. Some of the most selfish people have the most things and some of the best people always get the short end of the stick. The universe doesn't always play fair and sometimes it's downright dirty.

Karie is 55 nearing 56. She lives in Texas but grew up in Southern California. She was a virgin till she was 18 for no other reason than she hadn't met anyone that she liked enough to take it all the way. The big "homerun." She was a normal kid and liked to go out to parties and do all the things that teenagers like to do. When she was 20 she met some guy and they fell in love and got married when she was 21. Though the relationship had its problems because she was the breadwinner and would get frustrated with his careless spending and controlling ways, she decided that she wanted to get pregnant and stopped taking her pill. She was 25 and thought this would be a good time to start a family. She thought that in not taking the pill she would clean out her body to prepare it for pregnancy but after the first month of going off of it she was overcome with pain doubled over. This was deja-vu for her because at 20 she had gone off the pill and suffered the same fate crippled by pain sending her to the nearest emergency room only to learn that she had had a cyst on her ovary that had ruptured.

So now at 25 she was experiencing the same drama. She had been working as an accounting executive for Fiesta Americana and things had been going good in her life so she was surprised that she found herself in the same situation as she had been in when she was 20. At first the doctor's thought that she was having a tubal pregnancy especially because she mysteriously had tested positive for being pregnant and since she had good insurance with her job they went in through her belly button performing a laparoscopy to view her left ovaries where she had just ovulated. The doctors discovered a lot of problems when they went in and let her know the bad news. Her tube and ovaries were tucked up under her bowels and if that wasn't bad enough, her left tube was meshed together and sealed on both sides so that an egg would never be able to travel in or of it. It was shocking news that made her feel helpless. She told the doctor that she had always ovulated on her left side since she had started her period and always got really sharp pains during ovulation. The doctor decided to use a laser to try and make openings in her closed tube and separate the web of mesh that looked like a huge spider web. When the procedure was done he gave her a very powerful round of antibiotics to keep the infection she had from getting worse. The doctor told her that she had had a 4 to 5 centimeter cyst on her ovary that needed to be removed. He said the spider-web mesh around them was bizarre and that they had never seen anything like it before so she became the hospital lab rat with all the interns and other doctors coming by to see the phenomenon and she told me her condition was even written about in medical books.

After this she went home from the hospital and was hoping things would improve. Wishful thinking though because within a month she was in pain again and was given antibiotics. The following month she went to Cancun on a work trip but within no time she was experiencing the same old problems. The pain was gnawing and relentless so she had to stay in her room for four days before she could get a flight back. Luckily Mexico has pharmacies that you can get pills from without a prescription so she was able to get the same Darvocets that she had been taking back home before she left enabling her to endure the pain she would have felt on the way home on the plane.

Back home her doctor explained that he didn't want to perform major surgery on her because she was young and he worried about her never being able to have kids if he had to cut her open so they opted to have another laparoscopy that was supposed to be a 45 minute non-invasive procedure but when they started, they realized her situation had gotten worse and she was wheeled into surgery. Like a cold dead fish, she was cut open and gutted. They had needed to remove her left tube and ovary and when she awoke she was confused and in pain with bandages all wrapped around her stomach. Since her bowel was involved she needed to stay in the hospital for a week and was not able to go to the bathroom without the help of morphine and laxative type pills. Her hips were swollen and bruised from all the needle sticks but all she cared about was getting back home. The doctor instructed her that for a year she would need to heal from the surgery so she would need to be careful when having sex because there was lots of scar tissue and things had been moved around during the operation. He went on to say that after the year she would have a two year window where she might be able to still get pregnant but after that it would probably be too late.

Her husband and her were at the crossroads not knowing what to do because she still yearned to have a child and he was leary because he had already witnessed her almost die and he wasn't sure he could go through that again. One month after the surgery she was descending down her staircase when she got to the landing she was hit with severe pain but this time on her right side but that makes sense because her left tube had already been removed. She had her doctor's home number by now and called him immediately explaining the pain and later it was revealed to her that she had had a cyst on her right tube that an ultrasound showed had burst.

Over time she took things slow, not running, watching her weight, and not doing strenuous work but at 26 her marriage fell apart and having kids with him was off the table. The two year timeframe that her doctor had given her had passed and the years rolled by without any good news of a pregnancy. As she looked back on this, she told me that she wished her periods would have just stopped then because she had to suffer every month through painful menstrual cycles that seem now like they were all for nothing.

At some point she met a man who had three children and they ended up getting full custody of the girl who she was lucky enough to be able to be mom to for the five years they were married. She would curl her hair, play with her and the little girl would call her mommy. She said it was a very good time in her life because her biggest heartache of all was that she felt terrible guilt for not being able to make her mom a grandmother. She loves her mom dearly and her two brothers never had kids and she desperately wanted a child that her mom could fawn all over. During this short time of having her husband's daughter, her mom got to play with this little girl and get a little taste of what it would be like to be a grandmother because they all lived under one roof.

Today she is happily married and her dogs are her kids. She gets tremendous joy when she's with them and loves to spoil them and play with them. She lives on almost eight acres and wants even more animals like a little mini-farm. She is not envious of other people that haven't had the same problems as her but once in a while a commercial will come on with kids and it tears at her heartstrings and makes her a little weepy but in general she's happy. Lastly I asked her why she never adopted and she said that it was just too expensive and fostering was an option but it just hadn't ever materialized. She goes on daily accepting her fate and enjoys her life giving lots of love to her husband and pets.

PLAN B OR C....
When All Is Said and Done.....

River, Lane, and Chase at Angkor Wat

So the big wrap up. Someone asked me why I was writing this book one day recently and I thought about it for a second and realized that I had no idea. I don't even remember when the idea came into my mind but I was completely aware of the direction that it would take once I began writing it. I told myself that I want to have this done in a couple of months and away I went. I didn't have a computer and thought that it would be hard to type on my phone so my friend loaned me one of her old ones that had been sitting around her house but I couldn't get it to work and had to break down and spent the 300 dollars getting a new one. I've always been artistic writing poems from a young age and stories and have also gone through a spell where I painted everyday for like three years. I've spent time as a musician and I guess I just look for things to do so I don't turn to the bottle everyday like I had done for so many years. I need to stay busy to stay sane and as the days roll by I evolve as a person and a human being which I guess in the end, are one in the same.

In my personal life, I have experienced people who have tried to attach some false narrative to me because they didn't like me, were mad at me, or not happy with their own life. People will project their unhappiness on you to make themselves feel better about themselves and try and that's just the way it is. Your opinion better fall in line with theirs or it's time for the crucifixion.

When I grew up you were still allowed to have an opinion without being crucified. Comedians could save you from the humdrum of everyday life without being called racist, homophobic, and getting canceled. Granted, there were issues that society needed to address, but there was room for laughter and to be able to make fun of oneself once in a while. Cheech and Chong could never have existed today without someone claiming they were making all Mexicans look like potheads and others would say they found it offensive that they were stereotyping stoners as dumb. Chris Farley would have been attacked for being unsentimental towards fat people (or should I say people with a little extra weight on them) or you would have thousands of lawsuits filed for slander if you were one of those people who enjoyed living in their van down by the river. Richard Pryer would have had crack addict protesters outside his shows carrying around signs that said "Crackheads have feelings too." and chanting "Cracks not whack!, Cracks not whack!." And Jim Carey would have the Firemen's Union up in arms about his portrayal of firefighters with his character Fire Marshall Bill.

There is only room nowadays to be on one side or the other, no middle ground. Your group A or group B and if you step out of those two tiny boxes you will be considered to be an enemy of the state. I'm always willing to openly look at something from a different view. My views are fluid as water and I'm always changing my opinions over time because nothing is set in stone and I'm so glad I grew up in a time where technology was not advanced enough to pry into everyone's personal lives on a daily basis and tear them down by spreading lies and hate across internet sites. But love breeds love and hate breeds hate and I am fully aware that in the end we are all just like little ants scurrying around and our time here is just a mere spec on the entire historical timeline of our planet.

The Big Bang Theory states that the universe began about 13.7 billion years ago but humans have only existed for a blip of that. This theory became widely accepted in 1964 when cosmic background radiation was determined to be a relic of the early universe contradicting earlier scientists' views that the universe was infinite. Now it was determined to have had a beginning but the biggest question of all still persisted of "How, Why, and When?" Did some heavenly God create it? Was it created by scientific means? And just .08 billion years after The Big Bang our Milky Way galaxy was created. It is a barred spiral galaxy with large pivoting arms stretching out across the cosmos. About 4.5 billion years ago on the outer spiral arm of the Milky Way galaxy our solar system was a cloud of dust and gas known as a solar nebula. Gravity collapsed the material in on itself as it began to spin, forming the sun in the middle of its nebula creating our solar system that is made up of that star we call our sun, eight planets, and countless bodies; such as dwarf planets, asteroids, and comets. The inner four planets are often referred to as the "Terrestrial" planets because their surfaces are rocky. The four outer worlds are sometimes referred to as "Jovian" due to their larger size and are made from gasses like hydrogen, helium, and ammonia that make them unlivable but our our Mother Earth is aligned third in line from the sun making it the perfect distance away as to not get too hot or too cold and with the right makeup to allow for human life to exist. And bear with me through the next few paragraphs but I believe mentally reviewing the beginning as we know it helps us to move forward with more complex ideas and thoughts and if reading it bores you these statistical facts were borrowed from Morgan Freeman's Our Universe that might be a more visually interesting way to view and comprehend the earth's embryonic beginnings.

The Earth was born about 4.56 billion years ago.The planets were all moving in the same orbit when Earth collided with a smaller Mars sized planet and the debris from that collision created our beautiful sister moon. The perfect Earth-moon system was now in place. Countless icy planetarials bombarded the planet and that ice led to our earth becoming enveloped in water and in turn an ocean atmospheric system was created. Water vapor in the atmosphere then produced rain forming an ocean and the atmospheric pressure decreased. At this time the water was still toxic with high salinity and a high abundance of metals. 4.37 billion years ago the initiation of plate tectonics began where there was an upwelling mantle that displaced the oceanic plates above and led the plates to shift while weathered sediments neutralized the ultra acidic ocean. Through this process the ocean gradually became a habitual environment.

By 4.2 billion years ago a liquid core formed in the center of the earth. Convection within the liquid core created a strong magnetic field surrounding the earth and this geomagnetic field is what shields the Earth from the sun's rays. The earth's surface was readying herself for life even though sunlight was still not present yet because of the atmosphere but primitive life was about to emerge in the cave of a geyser when Uranium ore emitted large amounts of radiation creating a diverse range of materials and eventually producing the early building blocks of life; amino acids and phosphoric acids in a Nucleobase. Things continued to accelerate and bacteria became the first oxygen producer about 2.7 billion years ago leading to more complex bacteria and by .75 billion years ago It was able to grow in shallow waters. Soon you had the first land plants but they didn't have stems or roots to pull water to help them grow tall but by .423 billion years they did which are considered our garden variety of today like trees, grasses, and cacti.

Soon the single cell creatures in the water and land got more complex with the arrival of fish, insects, reptiles, birds, mammals, flowers and bees, and primates as well as our ancestors Australopithecus afarensis, Homo habilis, Homo erectus, Homo neanderthals, and finally our human species Homo sapiens that are all the people living in the world today that have, with recent archeological finds, been estimated to date back 315,000 years ago 100,00 years earlier than previously believed. So my long ramble was necessary to see that it took 13.8 billion years of cosmic evolution for the first humans to arise only 300,000 years ago. And look how we've developed in lightning speed in these years going from discovering fire to simple tools, building straw shelters to the pyramids, the wheel to automobiles to airplanes to spaceships to moon rovers. We've advanced in medicine creating miracle cures and vaccines, created calendars, and came up with technological breakthroughs mostly in the late 30's. Tesla who was a hero to the technical industry and his counterpart Thomas Edison brought us countless innovations like the incandescent light bulb, the phonograph, and the motion picture camera. Ben Franklin who had been a major figure in the American Enlightenment era made major advances in many fields. Newton discovered relativity and Einstein discovered E=mc squared, one of the greatest equations of all time which states that energy equals mass time the speed of light squared. In 1913 Niels Bohr introduced the Bohr model of the atom with a dense nucleus surrounded by orbiting electrons. This lead to the knowledge and capabilities to build the first disastrous nuclear bomb. But only in the last several years have we seen technology take off like at the speed of light. That has some questioning, "Are we getting ahead of ourselves?" Bill Gates and Steve Jobs are the founding fathers of Microsoft and Apple that have started a tech revolution that has led us to this super computerized world we are living in today. Will these advances end up determining our own demise? Will they end up surpassing the human race leaving us behind?

Scientists have been trying to calculate mathematical equations for years trying to solve the biggest mystery of life, the same one we all ask ourselves "Why are we here? What's it all for?" Life is so cold at times, it becomes hard to bear. Days drag into years as we grow from infancy to become bigger and wiser beings to then regress to smaller hunched over forgetful old people.

There are many theories like The String Theory that theorize that our universe has extra dimensions that lie curled up at every point around us. That's right, multi-universes. Galaxies are expanding, moving farther and farther away from one another, but why did they start and when will they end? Though our egos can be enormous and some might try to play God, we are really much more insignificant than we might want to believe. Granted one man or woman, with one push of a button, can destroy the entire world by starting a nuclear war but almost all of us are mere pieces of a watch where all the pieces fit together to make it work; cogs in the wheel if you will.

It has been suggested that alien sightings really picked up after the dropping of the atomic bombs at Hiroshima and Nagasaki, so could it be then, that any intelligent beings out there have intensified their visits to our planet because they see the peril we are in with our new nuclear capabilities? Who knows for sure but it is hard to believe that in a universe as wide-spanning as ours, that we are all alone.

Times are changing and perceptions vary from excitement to fear. Is George Orwell's 1984 going to become reality under the surveillance of the government or of one another? Afterall, every other house I walk past has house cameras leering out watching everyone's every move. Will our freedom of expression be wiped away by those with ulterior motives? Something that is a certainty is that mother nature has mastered reproduction through photosynthesis, her means more advanced than ours, while we try to learn how to be as perfect as her. Listening to the professor of theoretical physics Dr. Michio Kaku, PHD I was taken aback by his explanations of how we are creating a quantum computer that will find us computing on atoms that would be a huge advancement since the days of abacuses and huge Dell computers where Pong was the best thing going on it. Now we will be computing on atoms that could solve the origins of the universe and answer the "God question" of how the universe began and that is not to say that God can not be a part of the equation. The computing will be so powerful gone will be the days of computing with levers, pulleys and 0's.

We may end up in multiple universes because it has been theorized that every planet or universe goes through the same evolutionary processes from the simplest primal life to over time going through industrialized revolutions, scientific advances, space travel to developing the means that could end their world. But quantum computers will certainly take us to another level and possibly to another dimension. Electrons can be in two places at once and maybe we will find that we can too. The race to build these computers is on with IBM using electricity and China using light.

Just yesterday Elon Musk's company Neuralink was approved to start in-human studies that would enable us to use our brain for web-browsing and telepathy. Maybe the extraterrestrials have already mastered this because all accounts of them always talk about how they speak using telepathy. And quite possibly we will become products of accelerated evolution with the mixing of extraterrestrials and humans. A hybrid mix that some believe are already here living among us. Just today a car zoomed by me without anyone in the car at all. I'm sure soon all public transportation will be driven by self automated cars and I would guess our personal cars as well. I've often thought that cars would be self driven with a huge brain in the center with seats around it where one gets in and plugs in and basically accesses the internet or apps. and possibly visit other worlds virtually while the vehicle takes them where they've instructed it to go. The possibilities are truly endless and only time will tell the mysteries of the universe or parallel universes.

Will we continue to reproduce as we do today or will it become less personal where a woman does not even carry her own child? It's already changed so much with science making sex not an absolute in the reproductive equation. Babies can be made in test tubes so someday they might all be born in labs because after all ten months is a long time to put your life on hold being pregnant and quite often uncomfortable. And technological advances are resulting in astonishing results. Just a few months ago a woman named Mallory defied the odds and Savannah Kaplan explained in Health and Medicine that Mallory achieved what was once thought to be impossible when she gave birth to a son at UAB Hospital through the gift of uterus transplantation giving women hope who are experiencing uterine factor infertility, and really, it seems that anything will be possible in the future. Maybe with sex taken out of the equation in the foreseeable future, this will lead to less feelings of jealousy and competition. Those survival instincts or sexual selection traits might be unnecessary as we become more non-binary as a species how people that have had visitations described more advanced alien people as sexless. We don't have a playbook for the future so now we continue navigating through the waters of parenting that are deep and cold one minute, to flowing and comforting the next. We continue to ride the waves of emotion, anchoring in calm still waters whenever possible, to lay claim to our own humanness.

Having had three kids, I have gained perspective over time on motherhood and what it means to me in my life. I am so far from perfect but I can honestly die knowing I did one hell of a lot for people other than myself trying to keep my kids safe and happy yet at times I have, in fact, made bad choices. And really, I have shocked myself because I could have done so much worse. There were really sloppy moments like when I got drunk one time a long time ago and passed out on the cement by the kiddy pool in front or my house with neighbors probably walking by like, "What the hell," but shit who hasn't done that before. I've had wild and reckless times yet I've had times of quiet and solitude. "Life on life's terms," and anyone who's ever befriended Bill W. short term or long term knows that all too well. I mean, there's not too many people that have gotten arrested for drinking and driving the very first day they got their license. My mom had to endure so much crap from me. When I was sixteen she had taken me out to lunch to celebrate me having got my license after I had passed the driving test and that very same night I had driven downtown to go to a party in some dark and dingy warehouse. All I remember is drinking a lot and smoking some weed when all of these punks started going crazy throwing things through the windows and then proceeding to take a toilet and throw it down the staircase while it made loud thumping and crashing sounds as it recklessly descended the stairs while some yelled, "Fuck the Police," at the intruders that were dressed in black weilding billy clubs and guns outside the door. After leaving I got arrested for driving the wrong way down a one-way street. Thank god I did otherwise I probably would have killed someone or myself but my mother had to get up in the middle of the night and pick me up at Juvenile Hall because I was under age. Another time I had taken a combination of like ten different bottles of pills in the cubbard and went into her room and layed on her bed in the middle of the night saying I was going to kill myself but she did not budge. She probably didn't think I was serious and by this time, she was seriously sick of dealing with me. I ultimately ended up throwing up the random pills in the bathroom all night sweating on the hard unforgiving floor. Still yet another story of me peeing in a bush by 7-11 with my friend after drinking all day and eventually getting carried into my house by the cops while my mom watched my limp body pass by the front door entrance while being flung around like a sack of potatoes, arms flailing around like a dying bird. Too many of these stories for this book but there has been really good times as well, like watching my kid play soccer on a cold Saturday morning by myself as a single parent, taking my son and his girlfriend on trips with the family, letting so many of my sons friends stay over if they needed a place to stay if they were down and out no matter their ethnic background or their job status because I believe it says a lot more than having a bumper sticker or posting some IG post, trying to help some of them into rehab, driving across the bridge every weekend for a while to pick up an older Holocaust survivor to help her get her groceries because she couldn't drive, geeking out laughing with one of my kids, taking trains around all day to watch them skateboard, making sure they had food and a roof over their head, encouraging them to do whatever they want in life not worrying about being rich or famous but happy, being kind to others, taking trips and simply put, there are more good memories than bad. Every single parent I have ever met has told me "Your kid is so polite, so personable," raving about how much they like them so I guess I succeeded on some level. And both of my sons, who are now of working age, have jobs and pay their own way in life contributing financially to the family teaching them what it means to be responsible, the importance of being on time, learning how to take direction, and paying for their own college tuition. So I know that if we are ever in a bad place they will look back on their deathbed and know deep down in their hearts that I was there for them and that they were, "The meaning of my life," and I will be out there in some spiritual realm thinking, "Oh god, I hope I don't have to go back to that place again to learn more lessons!"

References:

Joustinf. (2023, Octiber 15). in Wikipedia.
https://enwikipedia.org/wiki/Jousting

List of Roman Deities (2023, Octover 26). In Wikipedia.
https://enwikipedia.org/wiki/List_of_Roman_dieties

Flood Myth, (2023, October 29). In Wikipedia.
https://enwikipedia.org/wiki/Flood_myth

Nuring in Medieval Times. (2020, May 12). In Rill News.
https://krill.com/news/2020/nursing-in-medieval-times/

Tharoor, Ishann. (2024, April 1). Before Noah: Myths of the Flood
far older than the Bible,
https://time.som44631/noah-christians-flood-aronofsky

Hayward, Laura. (2021, October 19). 7 Fascinating Acient Greek
Women You SHould Know.
https://www.thecollector.com

History.com Editors. (2023, April 24). Mesopotamia Civilization,
https://www.history.com/topics/ancient

Arthon U.S. History.com Org. (2023, August 7) Ancient rome. The
Rise Of the Roman Empire.
www.ushistor.com/topics/ancient

Kaplon, Savanna. (2024, July 24). UAB'S first uterus transplant re-
Delivers healthy baby

Ancient Origins, Praying for Life. (2013-2023). Top 10 Fertility
Goddesses.
http:///en.www.ancient-origings.net/myth

Bryson, Sarah. (2015). *Childbirth in Medieval and Tudor Times.* https://www.tudorsociety.com

Atsma, Aaron. (2000). *Hekate, Theoi Project. Greek Mythology* https://ww.theoi.com/Khthonis/Hekate.html

Hancock, Graham, (Narrator). (2022). *Ancient Apocalypse. Netflix* Rogan, Joe. (May 2, 2023). *Michio Kaku. The Joe Rogan Experience Podcast. 2 hours, 16 minutes.*

Balch, Peggy. (Dec. 5, 2022). *Witchcraft, Women & the Healing Arts in the Early Modern Period. Female Midwives.* https://guides.library.uab.edu/witchcraft

History.com editors. (November 9, 2009). *Cleopatra* https://www.history.com/topics/ancient-egypt/cleopatra

Hearst Magazine Media, (September 6, 2023). *Homer* https://www.biography.com/authors-writers/homer

History Cooperative. (2023). *History Cooperative. Ancient Greece Timeline* https://historycooperative.org/ancient-greece-timeline

Kokopelli. (November 10, 2023). *In Wikipedia.* https://en.m.wikipedia.org/wiki/Kokopelli

Lorenzo, Alis., Burns, Dasha., (March 15,2023) *Judge Appeal Sympathetic to Abortion in Consequential*

Mcculloch, Sam. (2023, April 30). *Twilight Sleep/ The brutality of giv birth in the 1900's.* https:www.bellybelly.com.au/birth/twilight-sleep/

Mundruczo, K., (Director). (2021). *Pieces of a Woman* [film] Netflix.

Reed, James. (director). (2023). *Chimp Empire. Netflix*

Cohen, Andrew. (Director). (2022). *Our Universe. Netflix*

The Economist. April 8,2023 The world's peak population may be smaller than expected

The Economist. Jul 14, 2022 The pecking order of the world's population is soon to change

www.ingramcontent.com/pod-product-compliance
Lightning Source LLC
Chambersburg PA
CBHW070752160726
48004CB00001B/160